Praise

MaryFriend Carter's The Fire is a Friend *radiates with the inspiring story of Kimberley, showcasing faith's transformative power. Through life's challenges, Kimberley's unwavering devotion and joy become a beacon, illustrating the profound impact of a relationship with God. Carter's narrative skillfully conveys a powerful message of resilience, love, and the peace that transcends understanding.* The Fire is a Friend *is a captivating testament to the strength found in faith, offering readers a compelling journey through the fires of life and the enduring light that emerges on the other side.*

Gordon Robertson, President
The Christian Broadcasting Network

The Fire is a Friend *provides a powerful message of hope and resilience. I was incredibly moved by MaryFriend's raw and uplifting story of how she grew in her understanding and intimacy with God through her daughter Kimberley's challenges. With deep wisdom and compassion, MaryFriend guides readers to transform their suffering into an understanding that God will bring good from all we face, as we shift our focus from worldly things to the eternal.*

I highly recommend this book to anyone who wants to be moved by seeing how He revealed His constant love and the good He brings, even from trials. MaryFriend's love for her daughter, insights, and practical tools provide a profound framework for embracing the peace of God and thriving even amidst the flames of life's greatest challenges. This is a book that has the power to change lives, and it will reverberate in your heart long after the last page.

Dr. Cheri Toledo
Kingdom Business Coach
The Created to Coach Academy

I have known MaryFriend Carter for almost thirty years. I first met her when she came to do a presentation to the teachers in the school where I was the Principal. We were in church together for many years and later came together with others to form a small house church. I say all that to emphasize that I knew her well—or so I thought. I had heard her share many stories about her daughter Kimberley and was always touched by them. She often talked about putting these stories into a book so others could find encouragement from them. God gave her the book's title, but it took many years for her to come to the place in her life and her heart where she could put it all on paper. This raw and beautiful story, straight from the deepest part of this mother's heart, will encourage you to trust in God and to embrace the story He has given you to live out.

JUDY DORRIS
EDUCATOR, PRINCIPAL
PASTOR OF LIVING WORD FELLOWSHIP

THE FIRE IS A FRIEND

Thank you, Gordon,
for your wonderful endorsement
of the Fire is a Friend. You
captured the essence of the story
beautifully. I pray the fires of
life you encounter will be comforting
and draw you closer to our Lord.

Blessings,
Mary Friend

The Fire is a Friend

Finding Peace and Purpose in the Trials of Life

MaryFriend Carter

Bestwine Press
Indianapolis, Indiana

A BESTWINE PRESS BOOK

ISBN: 978-0-9899888-6-5

PRINTED IN THE UNITED STATES OF AMERICA
10 9 8 7 6 5 4 3 2 1

Dedication

MANY TEACHERS HAVE influenced my development in positive ways—public school teachers, Sunday School teachers, and university professors. I remember exciting classes with Mrs. Bell, my kindergarten teacher. My final academic professor, Dr Massialas, was my dissertation chair and mentor who instilled in me a deep love for inquiry and critical thinking. A variety of teachers had a strong impact on who I am today.

The best and most profound "professor" I ever had, however, was my daughter, Kimberley. Through her life, she taught me to trust the Lord with all my heart and to seek His presence daily. She taught me to have Shalom in the Fire that is a Friend. It is to Kimberley that I dedicate this book, knowing that I could not have learned the lessons we gleaned together without her amazing strength and love.

Acknowledgments

ABBA FATHER, THANK YOU for loving me enough to choose me to be Kimberley's mother. She taught me more about the life You want me to live than I learned in all the years preceding her birth.

Thanks to my loving mother, Margaret Stewart, who was my confidant, my warring prayer partner, my friend, who helped me do life with Kimberley for eighteen years until God called her home in 2001.

My loving brothers and sisters supported me during times of trial, as well as good times. Bev, Jim, David, and Nancy are cherished siblings who, like Moses, held up weary hands praying for Kimberley and me through the years. Thank you for your prayers and sound advice as I wrote *The Fire is a Friend*.

Kimberley loved her amazing cousins, who gave her a sense of belonging in our family. Lindsay, Stewart, Aaron, Micah, Rob, Bill, and Matt, thank you for giving her dignity and self-worth. All of you made a lasting impression on her heart!

I treasure my friends who provided feedback on the manuscript. Thank you, Judy, for your sensitive editing, and Cheri and Jacqueline for your insightful feedback. Thanks to Mary Jo who helped add the final touches to my last draft, helped create the beautiful cover for the book, and saw it through to publication. To my home fellowship family and many friends through the years, thank you for your prayers, encouragement, and support.

Most of all, to my best friend and husband, Kelby, thank you for your unyielding love and support. I love doing life with you. As I was absorbed in writing this book, you patiently waited for meals that were often late! You are the best, and I thank God for bringing you into my life. Kimberley would have loved you as a daddy!

Contents

Foreword

THIS BOOK IS A MUST READ! No matter where you are in life, young or old, *The Fire is a Friend* has a message to impart to all of us. It is easy to look inward at what we are going through and think that our situation is the worst. I was told years ago by a very special minister, "Jacqueline, comparison is a sin. Often, we don't allow for growth in an area because we see others who we think are doing it so much better."

MaryFriend will show you from her experience with her daughter, Kimberley, that she had many opportunities to quit and give up all hope. Instead, she chose the better way: step-by-step and precept-by-precept to place her hope and her life in the Lord's hands.

Although she was a Christian when Kimberley was born, there were lessons she needed to learn. She even had to confess her anger at the Lord for what was happening to her daughter. Kimberley was a beautiful healthy baby until her first tooth started coming in. Then she went into unbelievable pain. That is when the nightmare truly began.

All the while, the Lord had a plan for MaryFriend and Kimberley. It was not the plan she would have chosen, but

His love and presence in her life gave her the grace to walk it out.

It will bring tears to your eyes to read about the many ways the Lord used Kimberley. She was bold in her witness and determined to share about Him in many situations. Only eternity will show us the true outcome of her boldness.

As MaryFriend was on the journey of praying and seeking help for Kimberley, the Lord opened many doors for her to minister to others. He truly was her Father, Friend, and Comforter. Out of her pain she was able to minister to others with the love and compassion of our precious Lord.

As you read, you will see the story of a woman who chose the narrow path. She had to choose between her child and her husband, who wanted no part in raising a handicapped child. Her choice was to put her hand in the Lord's hand and move forward, leaning on Him all the way. Was it hard??? ABSOLUTELY!!!

MaryFriend and Kimberley's story should confirm to all of us that *He who begins a good work in us will confirm it to the day of Jesus Christ* (Philippians 1:6).

JACQUELINE VARNEDOE
APOSTLE, PROPHET, AND AUTHOR
LEADER OF KINGDOM SEEKERS

Introduction

OVER FIFTEEN YEARS AGO, the Lord impressed me to write Kimberley's story to share the lessons I learned through her life. He gave me the title of the book that day: *The Fire is a Friend*. How intriguing! He made a play on my name. Friend was my mother's maiden name, and I am called MaryFriend. I wasn't sure what He meant by *fire* being a friend. I outlined the book and there it sat for fifteen years! The last chapter didn't come to me, so I waited. A few months ago, the Lord gave me the last chapter, so I wrote it first.

The lyrics to a Scripture song I love brought meaning to the message God was asking me to write through the life of my daughter:

Fear not, for I am with you
Says the Lord
I have redeemed you
I've called you by name
Child, you are mine
When you walk through the waters,
I will be there

and through the flame

You'll not be drowned

You'll not be burned

For I am with you.[1]

This song is based on Isaiah 43:2 that says, *When you walk through fire you shall not be burned, and the flame shall not consume you* (English Standard Version).

When I reflect on the promise that the flame will not burn you, I see the image of the burning bush that Moses encountered as he shepherded for his father-in-law, Jethro. One day while he tended the flocks, Moses came upon a *bush [that] was burning, yet it was not consumed* (Exodus 3:2 ESV). God appeared to Moses and told him he was standing on holy ground. The Lord then told Moses that He was about to deliver the children of Israel from bondage. God wanted Moses to lead them out of captivity!

Life with Kimberley was never typical, and much of it was challenging, as if we lived in a spiritual fire much of the time. The Lord continually taught me, burning out aspects of my character that kept me from being all He needed me to be. Through the fires, He delivered me from bondage.

Seeking answers and asking the Lord to move quickly to resolve our challenges was the plea of my heart. He rarely gave me speedy answers. Instead, He used each event in our lives to change me. My hunger for the Lord required that I let Him grow me *His* way and in *His* timing.

I've learned that when the Lord puts me in a fire or a fire comes from another source, He has a purpose for my being in the fire. Being tested and tried by fire was no fun until I learned to relax and let Holy Spirit accomplish His will. My job is to stay in the fire until the work is accomplished! When I jump out of the fire before I learn what He wants me to learn, another fire often comes to envelop me and teach me the lesson I missed.

Through the fires, he delivered me from bondage.

Isaiah 43:2, which promised I would not be burned, was interwoven with James 1:2-5 in my spirit. The Lord was preparing me for a walk with Kimberley that was going to be challenging and require patient waiting. Answers weren't going to come easily or quickly, it seemed.

Count it all joy, my brothers, when you meet trials of various kinds, for you know that the testing of your faith produces steadfastness. And let steadfastness have its full effect, that you may be perfect and complete, lacking in nothing. If any of you lacks wisdom, let him ask

God, who gives generously to all without reproach, and it will be given him. (James 1:2-5 ESV)

Through the years, the fire became a friend. I learned what Romans 8:28 means when it says *all things work together for good to those that love the Lord.* All things are not good, but the Lord can use them for good to refine us and make us into the warriors He needs us to be. In *The Fire is a Friend,* I share how the Lord transformed me through the life of my precious daughter, Kimberley.

Chapter 1

The Fire is a Friend

When you walk through fire, you will not be scorched,
Nor will the flame burn you.

Isaiah 43:2 Complete Jewish Bible

FIRES BURN. FIRES CAN be destructive and dangerous; fires can be cleansing and transformative. The Fire that is a Friend is both purifying and life changing. When we find ourselves in a fire, we can choose to remain in the fire and let the Lord do His work in us or to jump out of the fire, never knowing what might have happened had we remained.

Esther found herself in a fire when King Ahasuerus ordered young virgins to be brought into his palace so he could find a replacement for Queen Vashti. Esther went through extensive preparations for one year. When her time came to appear before the king, Esther had a choice. She could sabotage her preparation and act indifferently toward the king, thus removing herself from the fire. The option she chose was to remain in the fire by following her training completely. By remaining in the fire, she became the queen of the land. This ultimately resulted in the salvation of not only herself and Mordecai but of all the Hebrew people (Esther 1-2).

A battle for my daughter's life took place before she was born. Satan knew the impact her life would have on those around her, and he didn't want it to happen. The first fire I remember experiencing with Kimberley happened the day I discovered I was pregnant. My husband, Darrell, had gone to work at his law practice, and I was home doing chores. As I leaned over to make our bed, I fell to the floor in excruciating pain, unable to move. A sensation overwhelmed me as if a knife were stabbing me—in and out, in and out, over and over again—in the lower right side of my abdomen.

I dragged the phone off the bedside table to call Darrell and my doctor. No one was around to help me. None of this made sense. I lay on the floor in a fetal position, unable to think or know what to do. Everything was a blur.

On the phone, Dr. Sawaya said it sounded as if I was pregnant but that this was most likely an ectopic pregnancy. He wanted us to come to his office for a blood test to see if I was pregnant. Pregnant? That was something I wanted more than anything! To think I might be pregnant and could lose my baby was inconceivable! Darrell came home quickly to take me to the doctor's office.

When the test came back confirming I was pregnant, the doctor ordered an emergency sonogram to find out if the baby was in my uterus or in my fallopian tube. If it was in the tube, I would need an immediate therapeutic abortion; if it was in the uterus, our baby would be safe. Abortion was not an option I had ever considered, but Dr. Sawaya strongly stated that an ectopic pregnancy would be life threatening if left untreated. All I could think was that this could not be happening.

How could two people have such opposite reactions to this horrendous situation?

Going to the sonogram horrified me because Darrell's immediate reaction to our pregnancy was that abortion was the only option, no matter what the sonogram showed. He was upset that something was hurting me so badly, causing me to double over in pain at times. All I had ever wanted was to be a wife and a mother. This was my dream! My brain shouted, "NO!" How could two people have such opposite reactions to this horrendous situation?

I will never forget Darrell's face as he opened the car door to help me into the doctor's office for the sonogram. His expression told me one of us was going to leave the doctor's office extremely happy and one was going to be devastated. No news could please both of us.

The sonogram showed that our baby was safely attached in the uterus. What a beautiful first picture of our baby! That small, black-and-white sonogram image that showed a round light in my uterus is a treasure! Dr. Sawaya was amazed by what he found and had no explanation for the pain I experienced. He said an abortion was not necessary, but Darrell continued to pressure me in that direction. He wanted the pain to end! I looked at him differently, not understanding how he could want to end the life of our baby.

> ***When I look back at this time, I realize fire is what I faced.***

Although I had not yet been given the phrase *The Fire is a Friend,* when I look back at this time, I realize fire is what I faced. The choice that confronted me was to keep this pregnancy and have my husband thoroughly upset with me or to get an abortion. That was a fire that would test my trust in God as well as my relationship with my husband. If I jumped out of the fire by choosing abortion, we would have peace at home and my husband would be happy. If I stayed in the fire and refused an abortion, then our home might never be the same.

I was not in agreement with my husband. Being a mother had been my dream since I was a little girl. I believed the godly decision was to follow through with this pregnancy. Darrell reminded me that the Bible said wives should submit to their husbands (Ephesians 5:21-24). Submitting to him on this point was something I could not do because his desire was against the will and Word of God. My heart could not live in peace knowing I terminated the life of our baby for convenience. What I learned through this disagreement with my husband was lasting.

Are there times when disobedience is permitted in the Bible?

The Bible says that wives should submit to their husbands the way they submit to the Lord (Ephesians 5:21-24). It also says that husbands and wives should submit to each other in the fear of the Lord. Submission had been easy before I was pregnant. In this situation, however, submission was not possible. Darrell and I were a team. We became one when we married. We were supposed to agree on key issues before proceeding. My parents had taught me to pray about crucial matters until both spouses agreed. If we were both hearing from Holy Spirit, then we would hear the same thing from Him, assuming we were both listening for guidance. Directly defying my husband was not consistent with my character or personality; this was something Darrell and I had never experienced.

If we were both hearing from Holy Spirit, then we would hear the same thing from Him, assuming we were both listening for guidance.

The story of Moses's birth in Exodus gave me encouragement, as I turned to Scripture for guidance. Moses was born to Hebrew parents, Jochebed and Amram, during a time when Pharoah decreed that all male Hebrew babies be killed. He feared that the Hebrew people were multiplying and might become more powerful than the Egyptians. Pharoah ordered the Hebrew midwives to kill the male babies and to let the female babies live.

Shifrah and Puah were two God-fearing Hebrew midwives who directly defied the order of Pharoah. They refused to kill the boy babies, including Moses. When asked about their behavior and why they were letting the boy babies live, they lied to Pharoah and made up a story to cover their actions.

As I studied submission, I was amazed to discover that there were times when disobedience and lying were honored and rewarded by God. The Word says that Shifrah and Puah received a double blessing: they prospered and became founders of families for putting God before Pharoah (Exodus 1:12-22). They found themselves in a fire and were not willing to jump out of the fire to obey Pharoah. What a blessing they received for honoring the Lord's Word!

When Pharoah realized Hebrew baby boys were not being killed at birth, he ordered that all male babies be thrown into the river. Moses was saved from death by the midwives at his birth, but additional disobedience was needed from Moses's parents for him to survive being thrown into the Nile River as an infant. His parents hid him successfully from Pharoah's men for three months.

As he grew, it became more difficult to hide a strong baby boy. Jochebed put him in a papyrus basket and floated him down the Nile River. Again, disobedience in defying Pharoah's order was doubly rewarded. Pharoah's daughter found Moses and took him to be her son. She allowed Jochebed to nurse Moses and raise him under Pharoah's protection until he was weaned (Exodus 2:1-10). Moses's parents found themselves in a fire and let their character and obedience to the laws of God direct their behavior even when it meant defying an order of Pharoah. All of them could have died for their behavior, but instead God rewarded them.

Terminating our pregnancy was not an option I could live with.

This gave me great peace as I found many additional stories of defiance by people who chose to be obedient to God's laws: Shadrach, Meshach, Abednego, Daniel, and Esther, among others. God is a God of patterns. Scripture has many examples of people who disobeyed those in authority when they were asked to act against the will of God. Being willing to suffer the consequences of their disobedience, they often found themselves rewarded by God in the end!

That was good enough for me. Peace enveloped me as I shared my decision with Darrell. Terminating our pregnancy was not an option I could live with.

Pregnancy was hard. The first three months were full of pain and nausea, requiring me to rest frequently. Because I was in severe pain, Darrell had a hard time accepting our baby. He continued to put pressure on me, saying abortion was an expression of my love for him. He wanted me to be free of pain, and he thought abortion was a good solution.

Then, Darrell adamantly stated that if I loved him, I would abort the baby. When I refused, he began to reject me. He indicated he could not handle a sick child or the loss of freedom it would cause. Because I would not get an abortion, he argued that I loved the baby more than I loved him.

He took his argument further by saying if I loved the baby more than I loved him, then he wanted a divorce. He didn't want to be married to a woman who put her children ahead of her husband. I didn't see this as a choice of loving one more than the other; there was plenty of love for both. The stress on our marriage was almost unbearable. The fire was HOT!

The battle for our marriage was hard. We live in a world where divorce is easy to obtain, especially if you're a lawyer. There seems to be an attitude that it is okay to dissolve a marriage if things aren't going your way. Many believe it is no big deal to divorce and hope for a better outcome the next time around. Darrell's plan was to hop out of the fire if it got too hot.

I knew we could make it through this ordeal, yet his pressure for me to either abort our baby or give him a divorce increased. I said no to both. In a moment of weakness, I agreed to amniocentesis to find out if the baby was healthy. If the report came back that we had a baby with problems, I would still have the baby; he would need to decide if he wanted to share his life with the two of us. I agreed to the test hoping Darrell would stop pressuring me to have an abortion if we received a good report. A little before Christmas, Dr. Sawaya called to give us the results of the test. I can still hear his words as if he were speaking today when he told us, "Congratulations! You are going to have a healthy baby girl."

"Congratulations! You are going to have a healthy baby girl."

That night, Darrell and I named our daughter Kimberley Friend Shepard. Kimberley is a family name in his family; Friend is my mother's maiden name and my middle name. That night, Darrell agreed that he would give his daughter a chance and never mention abortion again.

He agreed to give us six months after her birth to make this family work again. He even asked if we could get a cat if we were really going to be a family with children. The next day I went to the Humane Society and found a beautiful black and white cat we named Tort.

As my pregnancy progressed, I continued to look to Scripture for inspiration. Abraham became an example for me in terms of staying in the fire when the easy thing to do is to jump out. He had a beautiful wife, Sarai, who was dear to him, but they had been unable to have children. Abram and the Lord were close friends and conversed frequently, and Abram (Abraham's original name) approached the Lord boldly. One day the Lord told Abram He was going to give him many gifts. Abram bluntly told the Lord that gifts were of no use to him if he had no heir to inherit them.

The Lord made a covenant with Abram and negotiated the terms, telling Abram he would have a child who was his seed and that his descendants would be as numerous as the stars in the sky. Then the Lord asked Abram to bring three large animals and two small animals and prepare them to cut covenant. (The Hebrew word for *made* is *karath*, which means *cut*. The word *covenant* is *beriyth*, which means *bond*. When the text says, *the Lord made a covenant with Abram*, it literally means that God cut a bond or a covenant deal with him.) Can you imagine cutting covenant with the Lord in person? The Lord put Abram into a deep sleep and cut covenant with him, adding to the initial promise that his descendants would receive the land we now know as Israel (Genesis 15). God honored and fulfilled this covenant in His perfect time, which required deep faith and perseverance on Abram's part. It was twenty-five years before Isaac was born to Sarah and Abraham, whose names God changed as a confirmation of His promises.

Isaac was the son of the promise. In Genesis 22, God tested Abraham. He told Abraham to take Isaac to Mount Moriah where he was to offer Isaac as a burnt offering to God. I often imagine the conversation Abraham must have had with God as they traveled three days to the mountain where the sacrifice was to take place: "God, You are a covenant God. You gave me Isaac as evidence of Your promises when we cut covenant. This can't be what I am supposed to do. It violates Your nature. It violates Your covenant with me."

No one would have challenged Abraham if he had disobeyed this command. After all, he could justify his action based on God's covenant nature. Abraham could have had a good life with Isaac, but he would never know the blessings he would have received had he been obedient.

Instead, Abraham trusted God. He told the two servants with them to remain where they were while he and Isaac went up the mountain to worship the Lord. He made a point of saying they would both return. Indeed, in Hebrews 11:17-19, the Hall of Faith, Abraham is remembered as a man who believed that if God had allowed him to sacrifice his son, God would raise him from the dead. God counted this as righteousness for Abraham. It had to be hard for Abraham to remain in the fire that day, but by doing so, he taught us a valuable lesson through his faithfulness. No price exists that is worth disobeying God. The cost is too great.

No price exists that is worth disobeying God. The cost is too great.

I told the Lord I wanted that kind of relationship with Him, no matter the cost. (Oh my, be careful what you ask for!) The walk has been precarious at times, but what a joy to fellowship with the Lord on His terms. From before Kimberley was born and throughout her life, our walk was one of being in and out of the fire!

Another fire began the day she was born—the battle for our family. On April 12, 1982, I woke up in the wee hours of the morning with a strange feeling in my stomach. My water hadn't broken, yet I had a feeling our baby was about to be born. It was a month too soon; we had not finished our Lamaze classes. I slipped out of bed while it was still dark to read my birthing books to discover what I was experiencing and if it was possible that this was the anticipated day.

Another fire began the day she was born—the battle for our family.

Darrell was sleeping soundly, even though he faced the most exciting day of his career. He was flying to Washington, D.C. for a few days to assist an attorney from his law firm who was giving an oral argument before the Supreme Court of the United States. Part of me didn't want him to go since we were within a month of giving birth to our daughter; yet an opportunity like this didn't happen often for young attorneys. When I woke him to tell him I thought I was in labor, we both thought this was most likely my reaction to his leaving town.

When I called Dr. Sawaya to tell him about the sensation I was having, he asked that we come for an assessment that morning. We left for our doctor's appointment with two suitcases in the car—one for Darrell to take to Washington, D.C. and one for me to take to the hospital. One of us wasn't going to return home that evening.

The day was bittersweet when our doctor announced we would be parents in a few hours. I was inwardly ecstatic; Darrell was distraught. He had not wanted me to follow through with the pregnancy, and now it was costing him a special moment in his law career. The day we held our daughter in our arms for the first time, Darrell lost the opportunity to appear before the Supreme Court of the United States.

As a borderline preemie, Kimberley had minor problems almost immediately. At one point in the hospital, she had a bout of apnea, meaning she stopped breathing. She was unable to suck, so I fed her with an eye dropper, using my milk that was extracted with a machine. We had a pattern: I would hold her and stroke her throat while the machine took my milk; then I would feed her. Every two hours, we repeated the pattern. After six weeks of being fed this way, she began to nurse. I was ecstatic. Nothing seemed to be wrong anymore.

Kimberley and Tort were inseparable when she came home from the hospital. She was so tiny, and Tort kept her warm as he curled around her feet while she slept in her bassinette. When I held her, Tort slept in my lap or by my side. He was her protector and never strayed far from her. Darrell would hurry home in the evening to hold her and stare at her for hours. He had a deep love for Kimberley. Our family was intact and good. It appeared we'd won the battle.

On October 12, 1982, Darrell came home from work to find a candlelight dinner for two waiting with his favorite foods. I was dressed in one of his favorite outfits and we celebrated Kimberley's six-month birthday while she slept in her room. As we ate, I reminded him of my promise to him that he could choose to walk away on this day. He was dumbfounded and confused. He had forgotten our agreement and told me he was as happy as he had ever been.

Our family was intact and good. It appeared we'd won the battle.

I asked him to make three commitments to me that night: (1) that he would never again use divorce as a threat when he was upset with me or the circumstances of our lives; (2) that he would make a commitment to our marriage for life; and (3) that he would make a commitment to marriage as an institution ordained by God. That night we renewed our vows to each other and promised to make this a godly marriage in which we would honor and cherish each other.

I prayed the fire was over.

Chapter 2

The Gift That Made a Difference

He will baptize you with the Holy Spirit and fire!

Matthew 3:11 ESV

I WILL NEVER FORGET THE DAY Kimberley cut her first tooth. It was not a joyous event. Three days earlier, we had celebrated her being ten months old. Life had been wonderful since her birth. However, words can't adequately describe the trauma that began with the eruption of that first tooth, nor the agony we endured for the next eight months.

Teething triggered excruciating pain so severe she looked as if she were having seizures around the clock; only they weren't seizures. It was pain! She would clench her fists, arch her back, and bite down hard to temporarily anesthetize herself from the pain, and her little body would shake. It reminded me of the Old West, where people would bite the bullet to relieve pain. I lived with a diaper around my finger, ready to put it in her mouth between her gums to keep her from biting through her lip, tongue, and cheeks, although she did much damage to all three. She slept little and had to be held twenty-four hours a day. She weaned cold turkey. After a few weeks, she stopped making noises completely—no babbling or cooing, no laughing, no crying. I had no idea what was happening to my daughter, and it broke my heart to see her in such agony.

Doctors were unable to explain what was happening to Kimberley. They had no idea what was triggering this pain. Research failed to shed light on the cause of her symptoms. Kimberley endured a continuous barrage of tests for this condition, including three CAT scans, two EEGs, and a video EEG that was sent to several medical centers around the country for analysis. She had tests for uric acid and amino acids, a skin biopsy for enzymes, genetic screens, and a visual evoked response test. All the tests came back negative. We documented 5,946 miles driving to medical appointments in Ohio over the next eight months!

I had no idea what was happening to my daughter, and it broke my heart to see her in such agony.

I wish I could express what I felt through all this. My heart didn't have time for feelings, as I spent every day keeping her alive! I went into automatic drive because of the exhaustion I experienced, sleeping less than two hours each day.

Kimberley completely weaned when this all began, but after a few weeks she even stopped drinking from a bottle. I learned how to feed her through a nasogastric (NG) tube through her nose to her stomach. That didn't belong in the skills of motherhood! Kimberley continued to regress and stopped rolling over or smiling. Her head rested on her shoulder because she was unable to hold it up. Having a baby who was totally silent broke my heart. I longed to hear her coo or cry.

Suddenly, I was overcome with anger—anger at God!

One afternoon I sat alone in my living room crying out to the Lord for help. Suddenly, I was overcome with anger—anger at God! I can count on one hand the number of times I have experienced anger in my life. It isn't an emotion I usually have, and certainly not something I had ever directed at God. Through my tears, I started yelling at Him, telling Him that He could stop all this pain if He wanted to! I asked *why* He didn't intervene. I wanted answers so badly!

My anger scared me so severely I called my pastor, Tom Collins, and asked him to come. He was at my home in five minutes and let me yell. His guidance was comforting as he assured me that God didn't mind my being honest about my feelings with Him. He guaranteed that God was not angry at me because of my feelings, and that He loved me deeply. We prayed together, and peace filled my heart. It wasn't just an okay peace but a peace the Lord gave me to assure me He and I were in good relationship.

Three weeks after this painful ordeal began, I received a phone call from my friends Marjorie and Marshall Davis. We were in the same fellowship and often had Bible studies together. They had attended a meeting the night before and were given an incredible gift they wanted to share with me. They asked that I bring Kimberley and my Bible to their home as quickly as I could. I had no idea what they were talking about, but those days I accepted anything my friends wanted to give me. I had nothing to give to anyone but Kimberley.

When we arrived, we met another couple who had been at the conference, April and Christopher Thom. Christopher led us in a Bible study on the Baptism of the

Holy Spirit. As he taught, I felt as if God had rewritten my Bible and was revealing truth I had never seen. This is one of the first Scriptures Christopher shared:

> *While Apollos was at Corinth, Paul took the road through the interior and arrived at Ephesus. There he found some disciples and asked them, "Did you receive the Holy Spirit when you believed?" They answered, "No, we have not even heard that there is a Holy Spirit." So Paul asked, "Then what baptism did you receive?" "John's baptism," they replied. Paul said, "John's baptism was a baptism of repentance. He told the people to believe in the one coming after him, that is, in Jesus." On hearing this, they were baptized in the name of the Lord Jesus.* (Acts 19:1-6 NIV)

I knew I received the Holy Spirit when I was saved. The Fruit of the Spirit was growing in me regularly. Not only did the Holy Spirit come to live in me, but most importantly, Jesus did.

Throughout my life I have experienced moments when it feels as if the Lord has taken a machete and cut off the top of my head to reorganize my thinking. The next verse triggered a complete paradigm shift in my walk with the Lord and caused me to reconsider much of what I thought I knew about Scripture: *When Paul placed his hands on them, the Holy Spirit came on them, and they spoke in tongues and prophesied* (Acts 19:6 NIV).

Marjorie looked at me and inquired, "Do you want it?"

I love to study Scripture. When I hear something new, my tendency is to search the Bible to find out what God says about the topic. I know people can easily misquote Scripture and take it out of context. After confirming the Word, I integrate the new insight into my understanding.

That day was different. I had done no individual Bible study to confirm what Christopher had said was accurate. I simply knew what he said was from God. A deep peace consumed me. All I could say was, "Yes, I want that beautiful gift." They laid hands on me, prayed a simple prayer, and I received the Baptism of the Holy Spirit with the evidence of speaking in tongues. I received only a few syllables, but that was enough. It was clearly a heavenly language and not something I made up.

Little did I know how much I would need the comfort of Holy Spirit the next few months and years as we struggled with the excruciating pain that was wrecking Kimberley's body. I spent each day keeping her alive. Prior to that day, I understood that God was a trinity: Father, Son, and the Holy Spirit. Abba Father was dear to me because I had a daddy on earth who loved me unconditionally. It was easy to transfer my love and devotion for my earthly daddy to my heavenly Father. Jesus was dear because I knew what He had done for me on the cross at Calvary and I had invited Him to live in my heart as a child. Kimberley knew Him too. Even before she could speak, when I'd ask Kimberley where Jesus lived, she would point to her heart.

Holy Spirit was less clear to me. Intellectually, I knew He was one part of the Godhead, but I considered Him a lesser part. I saw Him as a cloud or mist, something that was there but not tangible. He had not been real to me as God until I received the Baptism of the Holy Spirit. I didn't know how to hear His voice on a regular basis, so I missed much of His guidance. When I received the Baptism of the Holy Spirit, He became real to me, a real person. I stopped calling Him *the* Holy Spirit, and He became *Holy Spirit,* one of the persons in the Godhead.

Through my studies, I was amazed to find that God the Father is only recorded speaking audibly in the New Testament three times! Jesus spoke throughout His ministry on earth but not after He ascended to heaven, except when He appeared to Paul on the road to Damascus. Now, the

Father and Son speak through Holy Spirit when they have messages for us. Even Jesus spoke through the Holy Spirit at times. Luke wrote, *I have dealt with all that Jesus began to do and teach, until the day when he was taken up, after he had given commands through the Holy Spirit to the apostles whom he had chosen* (Acts 1:1-2 ESV). In Revelation, the Word tells us multiple times to hear *what the Spirit says to the churches.*

One of the first lessons I learned from Holy Spirit was to focus on *who* God *is* rather than on *what* He is or is not *doing*. That was a challenge because all I wanted was for Kimberley to be whole and free of pain. I really wanted to see God act. I knew God loved Kimberley, so it was hard to accept that He let her remain in such pain.

Obviously, God orchestrated the events that resulted in my receiving the Baptism of the Holy Spirit. He knew the walk He was calling me to live, so He prepared me for the life I faced. I had no idea how intensely I would need Holy Spirit over the next few years. God equips us for the battle He asks us to fight.

Kimberley loved to hear tongues even though, at eleven months of age, she had no idea what they were. Her little spirit seemed to know God was in them. My praying made a difference. When I prayed *out loud* in the Spirit, a peace would come over her and give her a reprieve from the excruciating pain with which she lived. When I tired from praying in tongues out loud, her pain would resume. Five of us in our fellowship had received the Baptism of the Holy Spirit, so the two wives came over during the day to help cover her in our prayer language so I could rest. We were still not sleeping much.

Something I didn't understand at the time was why praying in English didn't have the same effect as praying in the Spirit. When I held her body and prayed in English, Kimberley's pain continued. When I prayed in the Spirit, her pain resided but only temporarily. This conundrum baffled me. What I did know was that praying in the Spirit made a difference!

After three months, I called our doctor to say he either had to hospitalize me or Kimberley. I was falling apart physically from exhaustion, and she was not getting better. In May, he put Kimberley in the Care Ward of Children's Hospital in Columbus, Ohio where she received first-class attention. I was able to be with her as the doctors tried to discover ways to help her.

After we'd been at the hospital for a few days, April and Christopher arrived one night to pray for her. We had received prayer from friends and strangers, but the Thoms prayed differently. They laid hands on Kimberley and started praying in tongues, LOUDLY! I was horrified! Tongues were new to me, and I used them at home but not in public—and certainly not in front of Darrell. I had not told Darrell about receiving the Baptism yet, and only the Thoms and my four friends in our fellowship knew what had happened.

When they finally finished and left, I asked the nurses not to let the Thoms into Kimberley's room again. I was embarrassed and didn't want the nurses to treat Kimberley differently because they thought I was some kind of strange Christian.

How insensitive could I be, not wanting the Thoms in her room? Those two were the ones the Lord used to introduce me to the Baptism of the Holy Spirit, the gift that was keeping Kimberley alive! It took a few days, but I knew I had made a huge mistake! I genuinely repented and asked for His forgiveness, but the Thoms never returned to the hospital. I wondered if this was an opportunity missed, as Kimberley continued to regress.

At one point, the hospital staff asked the chaplain to visit me to convince me to let her die. I was appalled at this and defiantly said, "No." Almost everyone who counseled me agreed with the chaplain, including my husband. I felt completely alone. Kimberley belonged to the Lord. I knew in my heart that this was not her time to die. After twenty-eight days in the hospital, at fourteen months of age, Kimberley was sent home to die. The doctors said they knew of nothing else to do for her and they were unable to help us. They said there was no hope for her and tried to convince us to put her in an institution so we could have a *normal* life.

I knew in my heart that this was not her time to die.

All I could do at this point was to take my daughter home and continue to take care of her. At least the doctors had developed a cocktail of three drugs that calmed her a bit so she and I could sleep a couple of hours at a time. I gave the medications to her through the NG tube every three hours when I fed her. One thing I knew for certain was that other than the drugs, my praying in the Spirit was the only thing that calmed her and temporarily relieved her pain.

When Darrell held Kimberley for the first time the day she was born, the Lord changed his heart, and he developed a deep love for his daughter. Seeing her in so much pain broke his heart, so he began to withdraw from us. He could not handle seeing her so traumatized day after day.

When he was at home, he stayed in a room other than the room Kimberley and I were in. I was so exhausted, there was no fight left in me for our marriage. We were like married singles for much of those eight months.

I have learned to ask what lesson the Lord wants me to learn when I find myself in a fire. One thing I know, without fail, is that Kimberley and I may not have made it through this fire had the Lord not drawn us to the Baptism of our amazing Holy Spirit. He gave me peace during a blazing fire. He gave me exactly what I needed to endure, when there was no choice but to face each day as it came!

If you question whether the Baptism of the Holy Spirit is for today, let me assure you that it is. If I had no other evidence than my experience with Kimberley, it would be proof enough for me. When she was less than a year old, her body was wracked with pain and trauma as she regressed in development back to an almost newborn baby. I saw with my eyes that my praying out loud in tongues over her was the only thing that gave her peace and delivered her from that horrendous pain.

Give it a try! It is a promise of God in Matthew 3:11. *He will baptize you with the Holy Spirit and fire!* It will change you forever and give you the strength and power to face any challenge you may encounter.

When Kimberley was twelve years old, the Baptism of the Holy Spirit became even more real to her. We were living in Tallahassee, Florida at that point and worshipped at Christian Heritage Church, which had an amazing children's church. When I retrieved Kimberley from children's church on August 28, 1994, she almost vaulted out of her wheelchair. She hugged me with a bear hug only she could give, giggling out the phrase "I got it, mommy, I got it!" As she squealed with joy, she finally shared that she had received the Baptism of the Holy Spirit in children's church and that she could speak in tongues. I asked her to pray in tongues. She instantly became sober, gave me her precious smile, and began to speak in her heavenly prayer language: "Coco columba sa." How beautiful!

After that day, Kimberley's favorite thing to do was to pray in tongues. While she had an expressive language disability, her prayer language was fluid and grew. Here was another puzzlement. She might take ten minutes to express her thoughts in a sentence or two in English, yet she could sit in her room and pray in tongues fluently for several minutes at a time. Her sensitive spirit knew that tongues calmed her soul. I often sat in our living room listening to her pray in the Spirit with joy I cannot express.

Not only did Kimberley love to pray in tongues, but she also wanted people to pray for her. After giving a warm hug to an individual, frequently she would ask them to pray for her—in tongues. She divided people into one of three groups based on their response. The first group gave the response, "I'll pray for you later." This response frustrated her, and she would reply, "No, pray now." The second group would say that they are happy to pray for her. She would reply, "In tongues!" If they said they could only pray in English, she would tell them, "You need to get tongues." If their response was to pray in tongues, she was ecstatic.

* * *

Chapter 3

By His Stripes

And by His stripes (wounds) we are healed.

Isaiah 53:5 Amplified

WE HAD LIVED SIX MONTHS in a scorching hot fire with no way of escape. Fires can be hard to deal with by ourselves. Of course, we aren't supposed to deal with them alone. The Lord puts us in families, and I had an incredible birth family supporting me, along with a wonderful church family. I needed both!

Throughout my life, I had known God as a God of miracles, but I believed He just randomly handed them out. Each day, I pleaded with Him to choose Kimberley and let her be the one He blessed with a miracle. I believed in healing, yet before my eyes my daughter's pain continued relentlessly. The doctors told us that they had nothing to offer her. I knew her only hope was the Lord. Darrell's response was the opposite: "There can be no God if this is happening to our little girl."

Our marriage was under terrible strain. The more I depended on the Lord, the farther my husband drifted from Him. I was exhausted from the intense care Kimberley required. Darrell suggested that I visit my mother in Florida where I could get some help and much needed rest. On the way to the airport, he asked me for a divorce, saying he could not take this anymore. It was too much! Hopelessness, aloneness, frustration, and despair flooded me as Kimberley and I flew to Tallahassee. On the night we renewed our vows, Darrell had promised he would never use divorce as a weapon in our marriage. I could not understand what God was doing.

Why was all this pain being inflicted on my precious Kimberley? Why was God letting my marriage fall apart when I needed my husband? God could stop all of this in a moment, but He chose not to act. The devil was devouring my marriage and the life of my child, and I could do nothing to change either situation. As I questioned God about His inaction, He said nothing, but He comforted me with a peace I did not understand. Yet Kimberley continued to die.

My family and friends rallied around Kimberley and me in Tallahassee and joined in prayer for her healing. One friend devoted one hour a day to pray in her prayer language for Kimberley. The commitment of our friends and family amazed and blessed me. To be surrounded by the loving people from my childhood church was exactly what I needed. My father had been the pastor of this church until his death, and I loved the people in it.

Daddy often preached on James 5:14-16, and this was basic to my understanding of the promise of healing in the Bible. My family had seen many miracles through the years, and we believed in anointing with oil and praying the prayer of faith.

> *Is anyone among you sick? Let him call for the elders of the church, and let them pray over him, anointing him with oil in the name of the Lord. And the prayer of faith will save the one who is sick, and the Lord will raise him up. And if he has committed sins, he will be forgiven. Therefore, confess your sins to one another and pray for one another,* ***that you may be healed.*** *The prayer of a righteous person has great power as it is working.* (ESV)

One of the most spectacular healing miracles happened to my brother David, when a concrete wall fell on him and damaged his back so badly he could barely walk. He came to church that Sunday evening, and the elders anointed him with oil and prayed the prayer of faith over him. God touched him. David immediately stood up, touched his toes, and started moving around. He was instantly healed with no residual effects.

My expectation for Kimberley's healing was based on James 5 and on David's healing, only it wasn't happening. I didn't understand why Kimberley wasn't getting the same blessing my brother had received. Remembering David's experience from years earlier, I asked the elders of Mother's church to anoint Kimberley with oil and pray for her healing in accordance with James 5.

After church, we met in what had been my daddy's study. Three of the elders I loved from my childhood prayed heartfelt prayers over her and anointed her with oil. Mother and I could feel the presence of Holy Spirit in the room! At the end, the new pastor of the church prayed for her and then turned to me and said, "Don't expect her to get better just because we did that."

I had no words! Here was a pastor praying the prayer of faith with *no faith*. Could his unbelief undo the power of the prayers of three faithful men of God who prayed in unity with Mother and me? All I can say is that this didn't seem to be God's timing for Kimberley's healing, because nothing obvious changed that night the way it had with my brother. I learned to be careful about whom I allowed to pray for my daughter.

In August, my sister Beverley invited our family to come to her home in Houston to pray for Kimberley. Mother, Kimberley, and I drove from Florida; my sister-in-law and her three sons drove from Denver. Every member of my immediate family came except my brother David who had to work. He reminded us that there was no distance in prayer and that he would be joining in with prayers for Kimberley. All fourteen members of our family were in unity. Our prayer time was sweet and powerful. We quoted healing Scriptures, anointed Kimberley with oil, and asked God for a miracle as we prayed the prayer of faith in agreement.

We asked God for a miracle as we prayed the prayer of faith in agreement.

The first evening in Houston, my sister-in-law, Margaret, stayed up with me all night. I had not slept through any night during the six months since February 15 when this nightmare began. Around 3 a.m., Margaret had a word from the Lord that we were to take Kimberley to Oral Roberts University. My immediate reaction was "That kook? I'm not going there." After she assured me this was from the Lord, I told her I would pray about it. I had heard some strange things about that place, and I wasn't sure I wanted to take Kimberley there. (I have since repented and know that mighty works of the Lord happen there!)

The following morning, Margaret brought me the phone, saying she had a doctor from Oral Roberts Medical Center on the line and he had questions about Kimberley's medical history. After an hour of conversation, the doctor asked if we could be in Tulsa by noon the following day. In the middle of a hurricane, five of us set out for Tulsa, hoping for a miracle.

Our experience at Oral Roberts was miraculous, but not in the way I had expected. The minute we drove on the campus, Kimberley stopped shaking and became totally peaceful. The presence of the Lord was so strong that all her manifestation of pain stopped! The staff assigned a prayer team to Kimberley that never left her side during hours of medical examination. They prayed without ceasing and placed prayer cloths on her.

In the afternoon, they offered me a two-hour counseling session with a doctor who gave me some of the best spiritual advice I have ever received. I shared Darrell's request for a divorce. The doctor asked how I felt about letting Darrell divorce me versus going back home and fighting for my marriage. My reply was that I had no fight left in me since I was still fighting for my daughter's life daily. He asked me which option gave me peace. After prayer, I replied that peace came when I thought about letting Darrell walk away from us if that was what he chose to do. I will never forget what he said next: "Follow your peace. That is how Holy Spirit will talk to you." A burden left me at that point, and I knew we were going to be okay. To this day, Holy Spirit leads me by giving me deep peace when I have a decision to make.

After a full day of tests and counseling, the doctors at the ORU Medical Center concluded by stating, "The medical world has nothing to offer your child. Divine intervention is your only hope." Recognizing the huge gaps in my understanding of God's healing power, they suggested we go to healing school at Kenneth Hagin's Rhema Bible College for as long as we could. I had not heard of Hagin or Rhema, but I had peace when I reflected on that option. Clearly God brought us to Tulsa for a purpose. Our schedule allowed three days at Rhema.

At Rhema, God began a mighty work in Kimberley but even more so in me. On Monday morning, Patsy Behrman taught that healing was a part of the atoning work of Jesus on the cross. She taught on Isaiah 53 and focused on verse 5 that says *by the stripes of Jesus we are healed.* She taught that this meant emotional, physical, and spiritual healing. My spirit screamed, "Yes! That's right. Please be right!" My head said that *by the stripes of Jesus* only meant spiritual healing. Indeed, the marginal note in my Bible said "spiritual healing" beside Isaiah 53:5. Patsy went further, linking Isaiah's passage with 1 Peter 2:24, which reads, *Who his own self bare our sins in his own body on the tree, that we, being dead to sins, should live unto righteousness: by whose stripes ye were healed* (KJV). I was flabbergasted! It was as if God had rewritten my Bible.

I was in turmoil, remembering the advice of the pastor who told me I shouldn't believe James 5:14 would work just because we prayed it. The Scripture that came to my mind was from Mark 9:24 when the father cried out, *"Lord, I believe; help thou mine unbelief"* (KJV). In my spirit, I believed what Patsy said was true; in my mind, I doubted because this was so contrary to what I had been taught all my life.

Mother and I talked about this "new" interpretation of Isaiah 53:4-5 with much skepticism, trying to comprehend what we had heard. Mother decided to start reading the New Testament in Matthew 1 until she found what the New Testament had to say on this subject. It didn't take long for her to get to Matthew 8:17, which says, *that it might be fulfilled which was spoken by Esaias the prophet, saying, Himself took our infirmities, and bare our sicknesses* (KJV). God gave us exactly what we needed to open our spirits to the teachings of the next three days. We were able to receive the blessing of knowing without question that healing was a part of the atoning work of Jesus on the cross!

I was assigned two intercessors to teach me and to pray with Kimberley and me during the two-hour lunch break. They spent most of the time praying in the Spirit over Kimberley. During the first session, I shared about the preacher denying power in James 5:14-15, along with the confusing questions I had from that session. They asked me what my faith had been in when I prayed the prayer of faith. Was it only faith in the miracle-working power of God? Had it been faith in the knowledge that Jesus had died a grueling death on the cross so Kimberley could be healed? The prayer of faith suddenly had new meaning. That afternoon, for the first time in my life, I prayed from my spirit a prayer of faith that by the stripes of Jesus Kimberley is healed. I had done no word study, but I knew this teaching was from God. This message was for Kimberley.

During Kimberley's twenty-eight-day hospital stay in June 1983, I had been given a tape of healing Scripture songs. I played that tape in her room around the clock because the words grabbed my heart. The lyrics of one song drew me, and I found myself singing it throughout the day. I didn't have the title or know who the artist was. In 1983 we didn't have a home computer to search for this kind of information. I asked the intercessors if they knew these lyrics:

You'll never get Abraham's blessings,
with a Thomas kind of faith.
The mountains will just stand there,
in the same old place.
If you have to see it first,
hear it, or touch it, or taste,
You'll never get Abraham's blessings,
with a Thomas kind of faith.[1]

The intercessors immediately knew this song, "The Thomas Kind of Faith," and told me the artist/author's office was just a few blocks from Rhema. God used this song by David Ingles to prepare me to receive the teachings at Rhema. The prevenient grace of God had gone before me even before I knew I had a need. We went to David Ingles's office and bought every tape he had written or sung. I was arming myself for this battle with Scripture songs that continued to play in Kimberley's room twenty-four hours a day!

God always confirms His Word, especially when He needs to teach me something new that is a paradigm shift. I had so much error and so many gaps in what I needed to understand in Scripture about healing. As we prepared to go out to dinner, Margaret and I were freshening up in the bathroom, while Mother was with Kimberley and my nephew Matt in our room. Suddenly, Kimberley started crying for the first time in four months! I heard my baby cry! To this day I can see her propped on the pillows on the bed in that hotel room as I grabbed her in my arms to join her in the most wonderful crying spell possible! After four months of silence and inactivity from her, she was crying!

God always confirms His Word.

At that moment, I knew I was learning truth in the teachings we had heard about healing being a part of the atonement. The prayer of faith that *by the stripes of Jesus, Kimberley was healed* did mean physical healing as well as spiritual. God was equipping us for a battle we would fight during the years ahead. I had a new tool that would sustain me throughout my life in the advice the counselor gave me: *Follow your peace*. Peace filled my heart as I reflected on all we were learning at the Rhema Healing School, but I knew I would need more!

Chapter 4

The Nudges of God

For I know the plans I have for you, declares the Lord, plans for welfare and not for evil, to give you a future and a hope. Then you will call upon me and come and pray to me, and I will hear you. You will seek me and find me when you seek me with all your heart.

Jeremiah 29:11-13 ESV

OUR THREE DAYS at Rhema flew by as we learned more about healing than I had learned prior to this point in my life. We devoured the teachings and interpretations of the Word given to us. Despite my upbringing in an evangelical, Bible-believing godly home, I was not prepared for the transformation that happened to me at Rhema. I was overwhelmed by the love the Lord showered on me. He took me to places I would never have found on my own—places I needed to go. I had so much to learn.

As we packed in our hotel room to leave Tulsa, Mother asked us to help her look for her misplaced cameo necklace

Daddy had given her as a wedding present. As is my custom when I am looking for something, I stood by the door and looked around the room. A faint glow around Mother's makeup bag in her suitcase drew my attention, but I ignored this and helped look for the necklace. After thirty minutes of searching every corner of our hotel room, Mother found her necklace—in the makeup bag—in her suitcase.

Holy Spirit had shown me her necklace, but I had not paid attention or recognized it as His nudge. The idea that Holy Spirit interacts personally with me was a new experience, and I totally missed this nudging. I immediately repented for ignoring what He had shown me and asked Him not to let me miss Him again. The opportunity came sooner than I imagined.

At the end of Kimberley's twenty-eight-day hospital stay in May, the doctors had sent her home with a three-drug concoction to help calm her so we could both get some sleep. For three months, I filled a large syringe every three hours with the drugs, and then administered them to her through a nasogastric (NG) tube that went from her nose to her stomach. The doctors had warned me that this heavy level of sedation was dangerous. They cautioned me, "If she ever gets to the point where she doesn't need drugs, it will take a long time to wean her from them." To go cold turkey could cause cardiac arrest and even kill her.

We left Tulsa around midnight on Wednesday to drive back to Houston. Margaret drove first so Kimberley and I could get a little rest. Around 3:30 a.m., Margaret woke me to ask that I take over driving so she could sleep.

My next lesson in heeding the voice of God came at that point. I filled the syringe with the three drugs and attached them to Kimberley's NG tube. Just as I was about to push the plunger into the syringe to dispense the drugs, something bizarre happened. Much to my surprise, the syringe flew off the NG tube, spilling the drugs all over the back of the van. This had never happened before.

I quickly refilled the syringe with the three drugs and asked the Lord if He was messing with the drugs. *What is going on?* Hearing nothing, I attached the syringe to the NG tube and started to push the plunger a second time. At that point, the syringe popped off the NG tube. I caught the syringe this time, so nothing spilled, but I was baffled and thoroughly confused.

My heart raced as I thought of the words the doctors had shared about how long it would take to wean Kimberley from the drugs, along with the dangers to her life if I took her off them all at once. I spoke to the Lord, saying,

"Forgive me Lord, but if this is You, and if You are telling me to take Kimberley off her drugs, please do it one more time." I attached the syringe a third time to the NG tube. As I prepared to dispense the drugs, the syringe slid gently off the tube into my hand.

Hearing the still small voice of the Lord was new to me. I looked up to heaven and said, "Okay, Lord, I am releasing Kimberley to You totally. I believe You are telling me not to give her any more drugs, so that is what I am going to do." With fear and trembling, I woke my mother so she could hold Kimberley while I drove the next three hours. I told her what had happened with the drugs and that I had decided to take Kimberley off all her drugs cold turkey.

Mother began to pray and asked the Lord to put Kimberley to sleep in her arms as confirmation that what I thought I heard was from the Lord. This would be the first time Kimberley would have slept without drugs during the three months since she left the hospital in Ohio. Kimberley went to sleep almost immediately, and for the first time since February 15, she slept for four hours. God immediately delivered her from all drugs, and she did not suffer any withdrawal symptoms. From that point, she never again required drugs for this problem.

The Lord gave me a gift when we returned to Houston from Tulsa. My sister and brother-in-law, Bev and Jim, had a small group of their praying friends over to their home to meet us. They had been warring for us throughout this ordeal. We had a wonderful time sharing all the Lord had done in Tulsa. When the group was ready to leave, I asked Kimberley to tell one friend goodbye. She immediately turned to that person and smiled. Surprised, I called each of the ladies by name to see if Kimberley knew who they were. With perfect recall, she could identify each lady by her name. A deep reassurance flowed through me that Kimberley had a keen mind, and everything was going to be alright.

With perfect recall, she could identify each lady by her name.

I was excited and hopeful to return to Ohio following this amazing trip to Texas and Oklahoma. As Kimberley began to improve, I prayed that Darrell would be able to accept his daughter. She began to smile, babble, and laugh. Her sweet personality started to show. However, as she continued to teethe, we struggled with the pain. To lessen this pain and prevent more damage to her gums and tongue, Kimberley's dentist pulled her remaining teeth as they tried to come through. In October, when Kimberley was eighteen months old, he pulled her first molars. Overnight, she was pain free. We knew that teething had been the source of her problems.

The immediate crisis was over, and Kimberley's life was no longer in danger. The doctors warned me that she could be mentally impaired from all the trauma and drug therapy she had experienced. I saw no evidence of that as I looked at my bright, loving daughter. Remembering how she knew all of Bev and Jim's friends reassured me that Kimberley was alert, intelligent, and engaged.

The doctors warned me that she could be mentally impaired ... I saw no evidence of that.

Her laughter was contagious, and she loved to make friends laugh. She drew people to her through her gentle and sensitive nature. When I was faithful to listen to and obey His nudging, I watched the Lord bless Kimberley and me in ways I could never have expected. My faith and trust in the Lord grew. As I looked back over the eighteen months since her birth, I was amazed at the work the Lord had done in me.

Unfortunately, my husband found my faith offensive and wanted nothing to do with me. We had a collision of values. Having a daughter with unusual medical problems was too confining for him. He didn't want a lifestyle in which a child might hamper his career. Darrell carried through with his divorce and walked out of our lives, saying he did not want a Christian wife or a handicapped child. Even though my hopes were smashed, I had peace.

I felt betrayed and needed help desperately. Just when we were getting breakthrough with Kimberley's medical problem, our marriage crumbled. How was I going to work to support Kimberley and take care of her needs? She was still fragile, even though the teething issues had ended. I needed to be a full-time mother, but now I was responsible for everything.

Kimberley and I could live anywhere. The one thing I knew was that we would not remain in Ohio. My brother, David, invited us to move to the beautiful Colorado mountains on the west bank of the Continental Divide to live near him and his family. That was an invitation I couldn't resist. On October 29, 1983, David drove us out to live in one of the most beautiful places in America. My mother came for a two-month visit and ended up staying seventeen months.

The two years we lived in Colorado were a time of respite and recovery for us, and Kimberley began to flourish. She loved the outdoors and went everywhere with me except downhill skiing. She rode in a backpack when we went mountain climbing, cross-country skiing, or camping. Those mountains were exactly what I needed to rest and recover. The Lord began to teach me to trust Him in everything, and I started to recognize His nudges more easily.

I knew the Lord had a plan for us and that He only wanted good for us.

Jeremiah 29:11-13 rang in my ears. I knew the Lord had a plan for us and that He only wanted good for us. I purchased a small Christian bookstore in our little town of Granby. Neither Mother nor I had ever worked in a store or opened a cash register, much less managed a business. We were both teachers. The Lord used this as a private Bible school for me. I read every book and listened to every tape I could find regarding Divine healing and His Holy Spirit. The Lord used this time to arm me for the next chapter of our walk.

He taught me to trust Him with my money. Finances were tight. On Wednesday nights, we fellowshipped at our small church. One evening, when the offering plate was passed, I opened my wallet knowing I had one quarter left for the remainder of that month. Our pantry had food and our bills were paid, but that quarter was all I had. The Lord nudged me, and I gratefully put it in the plate. I remember thinking that I couldn't even buy a can of peas with twenty-five cents, so I assumed the Lord could do a lot more with it than I could. For the first and only time in my adult life, I literally had no cash!

For the first and only time in my adult life, I literally had no cash!

The next day, a friend from church came into our Lighthouse Bookstore. During Charlie and Cathy's morning devotions, the Lord told them to give me twenty dollars. Charlie asked if I needed it. My heart soared as a warm feeling and deep assurance of the Lord's care and provision washed over me. Later in the day, my pastor came into the store and handed me a twenty-dollar bill, saying the Lord had told him and his wife to give it to me! My little twenty-five cents had been multiplied 160 times in less than twenty-four hours! That day I met the Lord as my Jehovah Jireh, the God who provides all our needs. He has never let me down.

In Tulsa, the Lord nudged me to take Kimberley off the drugs she had been taking. The result was miraculous! Then, the Lord nudged me to give my last twenty-five cents to Him. He blessed me beyond my wildest imagination. All He wanted from me was obedience and all my heart! I have thanked Him many times for testing me and teaching me in these situations with His little nudges.

Chapter 5

The Word Works

But seek first his Kingdom and his righteousness,

and all these things will be given to you as well.

Matthew 6:33 ESV

A NEUROLOGIST CAME TO Steamboat Springs only one day a month for patients who lived away from Denver, so we made the arduous two-hour drive over snow-covered roads to see him in May 1984. He had reviewed Kimberley's thick medical file from the previous year. His thorough examination took approximately an hour. At the end of the evaluation, I looked him in the eyes and asked, "What is the bottom line for Kimberley?" Without a pause he replied, "I am not willing to say your daughter will ever sit, stand, run, walk, or speak." I thanked him for his time, picked up my daughter, and walked slowly to our car.

After securing Kimberley in her car seat, I began the return trip to Granby over the same snow-covered roads we had traversed earlier; only this time they seemed more dismal. Kimberley was twenty-five months old and had shown little improvement since we moved to Colorado. As I drove home, I was overcome with grief as I reflected about the ways our lives had changed in the past nineteen months since she started teething. I sobbed uncontrollably as the doctor's words rang in my head. This was not what I had expected to hear. I wanted a good report from the doctor!

Kimberley had never spoken a word. Because of the damage to her tongue, her speech therapists agreed there were many sounds she would never be able to make—if she did speak, which they doubted would ever happen. Many parts of her brain had shut down because of the intense pain she suffered and the drugs she had taken. The damage teething caused to her nervous system was extensive. She wasn't ticklish, although she had gotten her smile and laughter back. During the winter, she burned her finger to the bone on a radiator at church because she had shut down the pain center in her brain and didn't feel pain. She couldn't put any weight on her legs and her head still rested on her shoulder.

I am not sure how long I cried that day from self-pity, disappointment, and fear of what the future would hold for us. At some point, my self-pity turned to praise. I found myself singing a praise song from Matthew 6:33 that was playing on our radio: *Seek ye first the kingdom of God and His righteousness. And all these things shall be added unto you. Hallelu, Hallelujah.*[1]

Coincidences are rarely coincidences. I reflected on the words in the song I was singing and wondered if they could be true. Earlier in Matthew 6 was the Lord's prayer with the words *thy kingdom come, thy will be done, on earth as it is in heaven* (Matthew 6:10 KJV). Scripture told me that healing was the will of God and that there was no sickness in heaven. Later in the same chapter, Jesus tells us not to worry about our lives any more than the birds in the sky and the flowers in the field worry about theirs. I repented and asked the Lord to forgive me for being so discouraged by the doctor's report. I didn't know how to seek the Kingdom of God first when the fire that was supposed to be a friend kept getting hotter.

Circumstances seemed hopeless when I reflected on the doctor's words. Inside my head I heard Holy Spirit ask me whose report was I going to believe—the doctor's or His? I had no choice but to believe the Word!

I turned off the radio and continued to sing "Seek Ye First." When I got to the chorus, "Hallelu, Hallelujah,"

Kimberley woke up in the back seat of our car and yelled her first word: "Hallelujah!" Stunned, I almost drove into a snowbank! I couldn't drive! I couldn't speak! I couldn't sing! I had just left the neurologist who told me he did not believe my daughter would ever sit, stand, run, walk, or *speak* and Kimberley just *spoke* her first word, and it was four syllables long! I had a written assessment from her speech therapist that should Kimberley ever speak, she would never be able to make "L" sounds due to the damage to her tongue. Her first word had three "L" sounds in it!

How big is our God! This was a huge miracle from my loving God, Who gave me a warm hug during a time of desperation. At that moment, He deposited in me the gift of faith to know He had our lives under control, and I could trust Him totally. From that moment, I no longer needed a good report from doctors. *It is better to take refuge in the Lord, than to trust in man* (Psalm 118:8 CJB).

Kimberley knew something amazing had happened. She showed off her new word, saying "Hallelujah" to everyone she saw. She loved being able to *speak* to her cousins, Rob, Bill, and Matt, who spent many hours playing with her. She called me "Lujah" for months. Two more years passed before I heard the word *mama* from her lips.

The whole community rejoiced with us. A friend made a beautiful stained-glass *Hallelujah* to celebrate this miracle. It still hangs in my family room. A carved aspen log that says *THE WORD WORKS* sits on my bookcase to commemorate this day. I purposed in my heart never again to doubt the Word of God.

By Christmas 1984, the miracle that started with Kimberley's first word was beginning to grow. All four of her second molars had come in without excessive pain or seizure-like behavior. We lost a few nights' sleep with each tooth, but the pain did not trouble her as It had before. Dr. Robert Gardner, her amazing dentist during the eight months of trauma, wrote to me saying, "Tell everyone this is a miracle of God. I never expected Kimberley to keep any teeth in her mouth."

"Tell everyone this is a miracle of God."

Her vocabulary grew to twelve words, although her favorite remained *hallelujah*. She used a soldier's crawl to move around, as she couldn't raise up on her hands and knees. Her brain was alive, and it was apparent her receptive language was age appropriate. While she didn't communicate much with expressive language, she seemed to understand everything that was spoken to and around her. This was evident whenever the pastor told a joke on Sunday morning during his sermon. Kimberley would be the first to laugh.

Several years later, Kenneth Hagin and Patsy Behrman held week-long services in Panama City, Florida. Friends called me excitedly after attending Patsy's teaching on "Getting Mad at the Devil." Patsy wove Kimberley's story throughout her teaching, sharing how a mother, unarmed with God's full Word, struggled to save her child's life. We had learned much about the Word since leaving Rhema. Kimberley and I drove to Panama City to see Patsy the last night of the services. When Patsy saw Kimberley free of the teething pain and no longer being tube fed, she burst into tears, saying, "I never thought I would see her alive. This is a miracle!"

Through this wonderful season, I learned how important it is to speak the Word of God over my circumstances. *Standing* took on deeper meaning, and I knew I had to stand on the Word and put my trust in Him to act. *Then said the Lord to me, You have seen well, for I am alert and active, watching over My word to perform it* (Jeremiah 1:12 AMP).

Germaine Copeland's book *Prayers that Avail Much* inspired me with its Scripture prayers on hundreds of topics.[2] I devoured this book so frequently that it automatically opened to the pages on physical healing. Praying through many topics in this book taught me how to pray Scripture. I began to write my own Scripture prayers based on my understanding of Kimberley's needs. The key was to align my desires with the Word.

I began to write my own Scripture prayers based on my understanding of Kimberley's needs.

This is a Scripture prayer I frequently used during this season:

> *Thank You, Father, that the name of Jesus is higher than any other* (Ephesians 1:21). *The name of Jesus is higher than any disease, problem, or sickness. I thank You that the healing power of Jesus is flowing through Kimberley's body, for You heal all her diseases* (Psalm 103:3; Matthew 8:17). *Thank You that every good and perfect gift is from You* (James 1:17) *and that You desire that we receive Your gifts of health and eternal life* (Matthew 7:11). *Jesus's example was one in which He healed all manner of diseases* (Matthew 9:35) *and I know that You are the same yesterday, today, and forever* (Hebrews 13:8). *Father, I receive Your blessing for Kimberley, nothing wavering* (James 1:6). *She is free*

from the curse of the law (Galatians 3:13) *and by Your stripes she is healed* (Isaiah 53:4-5; 1 Peter 2:24). *Father, I ask You to hasten Your word to perform it* (Jeremiah 1:12). *In the name of Jesus, without Whom we cannot live, and without Whom we dare not die. Amen.*

Scripture prayers not only caused me to dig into the Word of God to see what He said on different subjects, they also strengthened my faith. I would read a Scripture and take time to meditate on its meaning. Then I would turn it into a prayer. Initially, my focus was on the promises of God. Later my focus shifted to the qualities and characteristics of God.

The Lord was gracious to give me a gift of faith to believe for Kimberley's healing, but I struggled in other areas of faith. I found the fruit of faith required that I exercise my faith. This often led me to question what Scripture meant.

For example, I was divorced from a man who rejected God by saying, "There can be no God if this is happening to our little girl." 1 Peter 3:1 says, *Likewise, ye wives, be in subjection to your own husbands; that, if any obey not the word, they also may without the word be won by the conversation of the wives* (KJV). Could I have saved our marriage if I had talked to him about the Lord more since he was not reading the Word? That was impossible in a marriage where conversations about the Lord were absent once Kimberley became ill. Indeed, my faith offended him. I could see no way my conversations would have brought Darrell around.

I asked Holy Spirit what that Scripture meant, and He led me to complete a word study on *conversations*. In Greek, the word *conversation* is *anastrofay*, which means *silent behavior or manner of life*. In 1611 when the King James Version of the Bible was translated, *conversation* meant *silent behavior*. Over time, it changed to mean almost the opposite. What this Scripture meant in 1611 was that the unbelieving husband may be won by the virtuous lifestyle of a godly wife, not by verbal exchanges with her.

I learned to go to the original language of Scripture when I wanted to understand what it meant.

From this study, I learned to go to the original language of Scripture when I wanted to understand what it meant. I was amazed at the many ways Holy Spirit taught me how important the Word is. Our Lighthouse Christian Bookstore was like a private Bible college for me during the two years we lived in Colorado. Shortly after I purchased the store, a friend came in to ask for advice. Her daughter was in a physically abusive marriage. They didn't believe divorce was the will of God, so she asked me what advice she could give her daughter. I asked her to return in a couple of days and I would search the Scripture to give her insight into what God says on that topic.

Believing God's Word means that we must decide to trust what He says about Himself in His Word.

This was the first of many opportunities I had to share what God says on many different subjects. During this time, the Lord burned in my spirit the Scripture that says, *The grass withers, the flower fades: but the word of our God will stand forever* (Isaiah 40:8 ESV). Believing God's Word means that we must decide to trust what He says about Himself in His Word. I began to make a shift from reading the Bible to find God's promises, to discovering the character and attributes of God.

The words we speak are powerful, so we need to be careful what we say. Proverbs 18:21 tells us that *death and life are in the power of the tongue, And those who love it and indulge it will eat its fruit and bear the consequences of their words* (AMP). Learning to say what God says and remaining positive was His requirement. I was tested about this when it came to Kimberley.

One struggle I faced concerned Isaiah 53:5 that says *and by His stripes we are healed.* I remember in detail the day at Rhema Bible School when Patsy Behrman taught that this meant physical as well as spiritual healing. I believed it as fully as I could. I spoke this Word over Kimberley regularly and integrated it into multiple prayers. Yet, every time I spoke this Scripture, I had a twinge in my heart that I was lying.

My frequent conversations with the Lord over this Scripture eventually bore fruit. "Lord, how can I say that *by the stripes of Jesus Kimberley is healed* when she is still sick and clearly not healed? She is nowhere close to the development of most two-year-old children." I was frustrated and confused. At times I felt like a hypocrite because I couldn't harmonize this Scripture with what I saw in Kimberley.

At times I felt like a hypocrite because I couldn't harmonize this Scripture with what I saw in Kimberley.

This battle between my faith and my feelings kept me awake at night, but it also kept me exploring the truths in the Bible. The plea of the father in Mark 9:22-25 gave me hope.

> *"But if you can do anything, have compassion on us and help us." And Jesus said to him, "'If you can'! All things are possible for one who believes." Immediately the father of the child cried out and said, "I believe; help my unbelief!"* (ESV)

The Lord understood the conflict between my belief and my unbelief, even when I did not. I asked the Lord to reveal to my heart what this passage meant so I could understand why my senses and spirit were at war. A dear friend, Ann Cope, uses an expression that conveys this perfectly: "The facts are …, but the truth is … ." Had she been in our lives back in 1984, perhaps this would have been easier for me.

The Lord understood the conflict between my belief and my unbelief, even when I did not.

I needed to speak like Jesus and say what He said. On Calvary, Jesus suffered and died for our health as well as for our salvation. Yet, His death and resurrection did not wipe all sickness and disease from earth. The truth is that He appropriated what is needed for us to walk in Divine health. I believe this. The fact is I do not see Divine health manifested throughout all believers. People I love get sick. Many are healed. Some are not.

The Lord gave me great peace when He spoke the following to me: "The outcome of your obedience is My responsibility." The Lord was telling me to listen to His voice and explore His Word. He was asking me to trust that His Word was true and that I was to war for His Word in our lives. He did not promise me that He would answer my requests the way I wanted Him to or on my timetable. I was to speak the Word to every situation and trust Him to do what was needed from His point of view. He taught me to give Him the credit for everything. If I minister healing to someone and they are healed, I am not to take credit for the healing. If I minister healing to someone and they aren't healed, I am not to feel bad or take the blame. The outcome of my obedience is God's responsibility.

The outcome of my obedience is God's responsibility.

Faith needs to be nurtured. *Pistis* is the Greek word for *faith*, and it means "a firm conviction, producing a full acknowledgement of God's revelation of truth." *Vine's Dictionary* indicates "the object of Abraham's faith was not God's promise ...; his faith rested on God Himself."[3] This was a revolutionary thought for me. While I knew Isaiah 53:5 promised that Kimberley was healed by the stripes of Jesus, the Lord didn't want me to focus on His promises. He wanted me to focus on my relationship with Him!

When I set my own emotions aside and approach God based on His will, peace fills me.

I learned to wait on the Lord to see what He wanted to do. When I set my own emotions aside and approach God based on His will, peace fills me.

> *"Because of your little faith [your lack of trust and confidence in the power of God]; for I assure you and most solemnly say to you, if you have [living] faith the size of a mustard seed, you will say to this mountain, 'Move from here to there,' and [if it is God's will] it will move; and nothing will be impossible for you."* (Matthew 17:20 AMP)

The key is to accept God's will and God's timing for your life. Only God knows all the events that are taking place around us and what our future will bring. Only God knows the work He will do in us because of the trials and experiences He allows us to go through. He needs us to align our words with His Word so He can work through and in us. I learned to focus on my relationship with Him and trust that His Word works His way!

Later in Kimberley's life, we spent hours in her favorite store, Toys R Us. We walked up and down each aisle looking at the toys, one at a time. She would choose a toy and we would "talk" about it to practice expressive language. She learned to read as she read boxes that held the toys. What amazed me was that she never asked if she could have the toys or if I would buy them for her. All she wanted was to spend time with me. This is what Holy Spirit wants too. He wants to spend time with us simply because we want to be with Him, not because we want something from Him.

I asked Holy Spirit whether quantity or quality was more important in my time with Kimberley. He gave me a new word in His response. He said she needed QUALNITY time. The quality of time spent is critically important, but children also need a wholesome quantity of quality time! He closed this conversation with this thought: "The same is true with Me!"

As I glance toward my bookcase at the aspen log that says *THE WORD WORKS,* I realize that its meaning has changed for me over the years. God's Word is neither a magic wand we can wave to get what we want from Him nor a formula we can use to manipulate Him to meet our needs. God is calling us to seek the Healer, not the healing; to seek the Giver, not the gift; and to seek the Provider, not the provision. His Word reveals Who He is. He simply wants relationship with us so He can pour out His love on us in His way and in His timing. *The Word Works!*

After two years in one of the most beautiful places on earth, the Lord nudged me that it was time to leave. I asked the Lord for a sign that I was really hearing Him, because I could have spent the rest of my life in the Colorado mountains with the amazing friends we made. I asked Him to sell the Lighthouse Christian Bookstore from one ad in the Denver newspaper. Sadly, I ran an ad the next Sunday. Two folks inquired about the Lighthouse. The second one purchased the bookstore, and thirty days later we closed on the sale of the store. With no idea what the Lord had in store for us, we loaded a U-Haul and headed to Florida where Mother lived.

Chapter 6

Abiding in the Vine

If you abide in me, and my words abide in you,

Ask what you will, and it shall be done unto you.

John 15:7 KJV

THE FIRST SUNDAY IN Tallahassee, Kimberley and I went to Christian Heritage Church because we were told Holy Spirit was active there and the pastor was exceptional. As we entered the church, I heard the Spirit say, "This is your new home. I have brought you here for a purpose." With great enthusiasm, we entered this fellowship, and I sat under the most anointed pastor-teacher-prophet of my life, Pastor Robert Shelley, whom I came to know as Shelley. I thought Tallahassee was to be only a short visit with Mother, but it turned out to be our resting place for the next ten years.

One Sunday evening, our associate pastor, Johnny Swails, taught on the presence of God and hearing the voice of Holy Spirit. He instructed us that Holy Spirit wants to speak to us daily and that we should expect this in our walk with Him. He explained that the only way we can lead a Spirit-led life is to know and follow the voice of Holy Spirit. The Lord wants to pour out His Spirit on us!

My life was transformed that night as I finally understood that Holy Spirit is as much God as are the Father and the Son! How had I missed this all my life? Holy Spirit Is the power of the Trinity. He is my teacher, my comforter, my companion. My parents had taught me to pray to the Father, in the name of Jesus, by the power of Holy Spirit. For the first time, that made sense to me.

After a short but life-changing teaching on Holy Spirit, Johnny Swails dimmed the lights in the prayer room and asked us to close our eyes so we could focus on Holy Spirit. One at a time, he asked us four questions for which we already knew the answer. He wanted us to sit quietly and listen to how Holy Spirit would tell us the answer.

The first question was "Are you here, Holy Spirit?" We sat quietly for about five minutes until all of us had an answer. We shared what we heard and how we knew it was Holy Spirit. I heard Him say, "Yes, I am here." The sound was inside my head, and you would not have heard Him had you been sitting beside me. But He did something else! I had a sensation in my throat like the one I had in junior high when a boy I liked walked into a room. I wondered if this would be a pattern He would use again.

The second question was "Do you love me?" We sat quietly for another five minutes and shared what we heard. Pastor Swails wanted to know how we knew it was Holy Spirit. Inside my head I heard Him say, "Yes, I love you," and that tingling feeling in my neck returned. This was exciting!

We all heard a response much more quickly to the third question, "Are you pleased with me?" After we shared what we heard with this question, Pastor Swails asked the hardest question. "Tell me something you want me to do this week." This took longer, but we all received an assignment from Holy Spirit. For each of the four questions, I felt that special feeling just before Holy Spirit spoke to me. How incredible that He wanted to fellowship and communicate with me this way!

How incredible that He wanted to fellowship and communicate with me this way!

I decided to continue to practice hearing His voice. Each day for a couple of weeks, I would go to my closet and ask Holy Spirit what He wanted me to wear that day. Some days He would tell me to dress casually; other days He suggested that I dress in Sunday clothes. On a couple of days, I literally saw a glow around a specific outfit, so I wore it. On some days He was silent, and I chose what I wanted to wear.

The amazing thing was that I discovered why I was wearing the clothes He chose each day. For example, one day when I was in super-casual clothes, I went shopping in a local department store. A stranger approached me who looked like she was homeless. We were able to talk about her needs, and she let me pray for her. I believe she might not have approached me had I been overdressed that day.

It also amazes me that the special tingling feeling has continued to come after almost forty years! If I get busy and don't spend time with Holy Spirit, I soon realize I am missing His touch when there is no manifestation of that feeling. The absence of His touch is a special message that I am not doing what I should be doing to stay intimate with Him.

One particularly challenging day, frustration and exhaustion overwhelmed me as I reflected on the fact that we were still struggling with many of the same issues we had been facing for seven years. Kimberley had a bad day with much inappropriate behavior stemming from being in so much pain. The medical world had no answers for us, and prayer didn't seem to be working!

After tucking Kimberley safely into her bed and seeing she was at peace in her sleep, I went to my room to have a conversation with the Lord. I liked talking to the Lord at my computer. I could journal the questions I was asking, as well as what He was saying to me in those moments. This conversation is one I will never forget, as it had life-changing implications for me and little to do with Kimberley. To this day, I can reexperience the emotions and feelings from this interaction with the Lord.

Lord, why isn't Kimberley healed?

As I sat at the computer, I typed my question that was a cry to the Lord for help. "Lord, why isn't Kimberley healed?" Then I expressed my heart to Him out loud. "Your Word says in John 15:7 that *I can ask whatever I want, and it will happen.* Doesn't that mean You want to give me anything I need if it lines up with Your Word? You said in Isaiah 53:5 *by the stripes of Jesus we are healed,* and in 1 Peter 2:23 *by the stripes of Jesus we were healed.* Jesus took the stripes and beating He suffered so we can walk in Divine health. You have revealed yourself as Jehovah Rapha, the God who heals all manner of diseases. Your promises are true. You are healer. I believe I can ask for healing for Kimberley based on your Word."

Ask is such an interesting word in Greek. *Aiteo*[1] means to respectfully demand or beg from someone who has authority over you something that is due or rightfully owed to you, expecting to receive what you ask for. The same word is used when Jesus tells us, "*Keep asking, and it will be given to you; keep seeking, and you will find; keep knocking, and the door will be opened to you. For everyone who keeps asking receives; he who keeps seeking finds; and to him who keeps knocking, the door will be opened*" (Matthew 7:7-8 CJB). One should expect to receive what one asks for when it is promised in God's Word.

I was asking, but Kimberley was not receiving.

Inside my head I heard the voice of Holy Spirit speak to me. He asked a simple question: ***Why do you want her healed?*** Immediately my brain was flooded with four reasons why I wanted her healed.

First, I wanted Kimberley to be able to play with other children freely. My heart broke at times when I saw the look in her eyes as she watched other children run, dance, and play games with each other. Children would come over to her wheelchair for a few minutes to chat but then rush off to do more lively activities. I wanted my daughter to have a complete and active childhood like other children, full of many adventures she was missing. In Colorado, I could put her in a backpack and take her skiing when she was two years old. Now that she was seven, we were more limited in what we could do.

Second, I desired a godly husband who could be a part of our lives. I wanted a man who could love Kimberley just the way she was yet believe for a healing miracle. I longed for a mate who could share this walk with me. Several men had come into our lives, but they didn't want the commitment that a child with multiple disabilities would require. Being rejected by men would less likely be an issue if she were whole.

Third, what a blessing it would be when a child with multiple disabilities who struggled with expressive language, along with sensory and physical issues, could give her testimony to the miracle-working, healing power of Jesus! Kimberley was joyful and laughed easily with a laughter that made others join in. People were drawn to her, but they didn't know how to interact with her. Her faith was solid, and her life was a testimony to the wonderful Lord we served. I knew her testimony would be one that would draw others to Jesus and cause them to want to grow deeper in their relationship with Him. What a powerhouse she would be in the Kingdom of God.

Fourth, it would be for Your glory, Lord. I didn't really understand what this meant, but I knew men glorified God when Jesus healed the paralyzed man whose friends let him down through the roof in Mark 2.

> John 15:7-8 (KJV) had these words: *If you abide in me, and my words abide in you, Ask what you will, and it shall be done unto you. By this my Father is glorified, that you bear much fruit and so prove to be my disciples.*

I knew the Lord would be glorified in her healing miracle and that she would bear much fruit.

As soon as I finished sharing the four reasons why I wanted Kimberley to be healed, Holy Spirit spoke again, causing me to catch my breath. He said, "The first three reasons are sin and must go. You must want her healing only for My glory. Let's talk about abiding."

The first half of John 15:7 says, *"If you abide in me and [if] my words abide in you ..."* There was that conditional clause *if ..., then*. This was a conditional promise and this verse required two *ifs*: that I abide in Jesus and that His rhema words abide in me. Learning the power of abiding has been my life mission.

John 15 through 17 contains some of the last recorded words of Jesus before He and His disciples left the Last Supper to go to the Garden of Gethsemane to pray. Jesus knew what was coming that night with His impending arrest and trial, followed by a horrendous crucifixion the next day. That He chose to talk about abiding that night tells us that He considers this to be a critical aspect of our walk with Him.

The Lord gave me a visual to show how basic abiding is to my walk with Him.

The Lord gave me a visual to show how basic abiding is to my walk with Him. He showed me a stack of antique alphabet blocks with *A B C D E* stacked. Holy Spirit said that the ABCs are fundamental to my ability to read.

Then I saw His hand take a bunch of grapes and cover the *C* with them. He took a sixth block with an *I* and placed it over the top of the stack to form the word *ABIDE*. The message was clear, and I had a deep knowing in my spirit that abiding was as essential to my walk of faith as the ABCs were to my ability to read. The Lord was calling me to a walk, and the key was to abide.

Abide is *meno* in Greek and means *steadfastly, continuously, rooted, unmoving, and stable.*[2] *Meno* means that I choose to be constantly attached to the Vine no matter what the circumstances of our lives are. To abide meant I had to decide to believe based on the Word of God rather than on what I was experiencing. I paraphrased my view of this verse to read as follows:

If I steadfastly and continuously remain constantly unmoving, rooted, and united with Jesus, and if His rhema words steadfastly and continuously remain and abide rooted deep in me, then I can ask whatever I want that lines up with the Word of God, and it will happen.

This changed my perspective of the things I asked God. To ask for the will of God and receive it is one part of a walk of faith, but this is a conditional *if-then* verse. *If* I abide in Him and *if* His rhema words abide in me, *then* my life will be totally connected to the Vine, and I can live in the will of God for my life—whatever that means. I wanted to bear fruit, which meant the Lord was going to prune me. This meant He was going to cleanse me. Bearing fruit in my life meant abiding in the Vine and discovering His will for my life.

Pruning happens in the fire that is a friend. As He burns my selfish will out of me and helps it conform to His will, the fruit I bear will be productive. Yet He promises that as we bear fruit, He will continue to prune us so we can bear more fruit (John 15:2). If we choose not to abide in Him, then He promises we will be like unproductive branches that are thrown away, dried up, flung into a fire where they are burned up (John 15:6). These are hard words but ones the Lord chose to share with His disciples on the last night before His crucifixion. I knew I had to pay attention and try to live by them, making John 15:7 my life verse.

A few years ago, I planted a ruby red grapefruit tree in our backyard. A couple of years passed before it produced fruit. The third year, I watched the tree daily as two grapefruit ripened slowly. No amount of willing it to ripen faster worked; nor could the fruit tell the tree how to ripen it more quickly. The tree sent the juices to the grapefruit, and it ripened in due season. So it is with us and our Vine, Jesus. He ripens us; He works in us; He directs our paths through Holy Spirit.

What I learned in this encounter with Holy Spirit was another lesson that the Fire is a Friend. The Lord had a plan for Kimberley and me that was different from my plan. In my mind, after Kimberley received her miracle, I could see her sharing her testimony in churches and leading hundreds of people to the Lord. She loved to witness in her non-verbal ways. Imagine what she would do with full speech! There would be no stopping the impact of her life once she was healed!

God was not going to work those miracles for us in the way I was asking. He was showing me that our part in His plan was bigger than our knowing Him only as a miracle-working God. I had pleaded with the Lord to give

Kimberley a miracle so she could be *normal* and live a *normal* life. That was not His plan for us.

If God had given us the miracle of total physical restoration at this point of Kimberley's life, our testimony would have been to the wonderful miracle-working power of God. We would have encouraged others to seek His miracles for their lives. We would have missed the greatness of His plan for what He wanted to accomplish through us in His Kingdom purpose in our lives.

Had He given us the miracle I begged for, I might never have learned what faith requires! I might never have learned what it means to abide in the middle of the fire! God is so much bigger than His miracles, yet when He sends them, they are wonderful. We had many along the way.

I was reminded of the three days we spent at Rhema Bible School when Kimberley was a baby. It was there that I learned Divine healing was a part of the atoning work of Jesus on the cross. Something that puzzled me was that multiple people at Rhema asked me if I could *stand*. I had no idea what they meant as they shared another Biblical concept for me.

Ephesians 6:13-14 (CJB) says, *So take up every piece of war equipment God provides; so that when the evil day comes, you will be able to resist; and when the battle is won, you will still be standing. Therefore, stand!* To stand means to continue, to endure, or to persist. I learned that soldiers in biblical times readied themselves for battle and then stood waiting for orders. I remember thinking, "I don't want to stand. I want a miracle. I want this pain to end. I want my baby healed."

Abiding was another lesson in *standing*. He taught me to seek the Healer, not the healing. My relationship with Him was more important than His making my life easier through the miracle I wanted. He taught me that abiding in the vine was the key to victorious living.

I learned to ask what desires in my life were keeping me from completely, steadfastly, and continuously abiding in the Lord so I could receive rhema words from Him. I love to study the Word. When Holy Spirit takes a Scripture off the written page and burns it in my heart, I am changed.

As I studied abiding (*meno*), the Lord took me to a powerful Greek word that became critical in my walk: *hupomeno*.[3] Adding *hupo* to *meno* was another breath-taking moment! *Hupo* includes two aspects of the walk to which the Lord was calling Kimberley and me. The first part of *hupo* meant being under a hard time and carrying a heavy load.

To say this described our lives was an understatement. The second half of *hupo* meant that I would not be moved from the conviction that God is in charge and has a plan. I am where I am supposed to be, doing what I am supposed to be doing. An energizing hope came when Holy Spirit gave rhema insight into *hupomeno.* I learned that abiding in the Vine would encompass carrying a load that would strengthen my faith as we lived out the Lord's will for our lives.

Hupomeno taught me to endure and to know that I needed a tenacious, persistent, uncompromising spirit. I learned how near the Lord is in the fire. Isaiah 41:10 says, *Don't be afraid, for I am with you; don't be distressed, for I am your God. I give you strength, I give you help, I support you with my victorious right hand* (CJB). The Lord was calling me to live in such a way that all glory was His. He wanted me to learn many lessons in this fire and not to jump out of the fire to have an easier life. I had to choose His way!

I learned how near the Lord is in the fire.

By teaching me *hupomeno,* the Lord showed me I would have a life others perceived as hard. For me, the burden was lifted. I experienced what it means to carry a load that the Lord asks you to carry. These are powerful and liberating words the Lord spoke:

> *Come to me, all of you who are struggling and burdened, and I will give you rest. Take my yoke upon you and learn from me, because I am gentle and humble in heart, and you will find rest for your souls. For my yoke is easy, and my burden is light.* (Matthew 11:28-30 CJB)

When I accepted that the life Kimberley and I were going to live was going to be different from most, it became joy!

The lesson of abiding in the vine meant trusting the goodness of God and rejoicing in His love! Romans 12:12 CJB tells us, *Rejoice in hope, be patient in tribulation, be constant in prayer.* The freedom that comes in abiding is powerful through submission to the will of God. I had deep peace when I accepted that we were where Holy Spirit needed us to be, living the life the Lord chose for us—that was enough.

Kimberley happy and healthy, before teething

Seeing angels

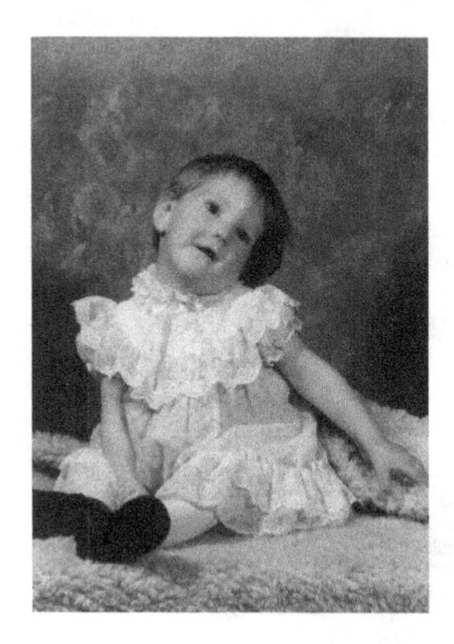

Kimberley, age two

Cross-country skiing

Kimberley and Mom

Kimberley and Grandma

Riding a carousel

Now for the real horse!

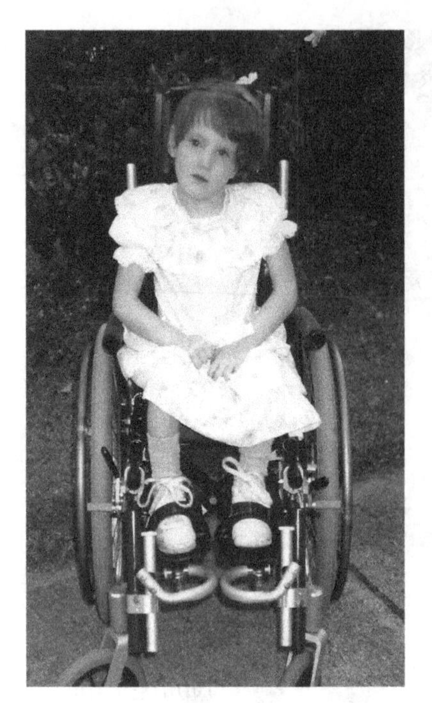

First wheelchair

Kimberley in tallit
(Jewish prayer shawl)

A ball bath for relaxation

Carved aspen log: The Word Works

Ready for the middle school Valentine Dance

Chapter 7

Job's Friends

For consider your calling, brothers: not many of you were wise according to worldly standards, not many were powerful, not many were of noble birth. But God chose what is foolish in the world to shame the wise; God chose what is weak in the world to shame the strong; God chose what is low and despised in the world, even things that are not, to bring to nothing things that are, so that no human being might boast in the presence of God.

1 Corinthians 1:26-29 ESV

I HAD NEVER SPENT ANY TIME with people with disabilities before my daughter was born. When Kimberley's development stopped at six months and the teething pain began four months later, I was totally unprepared for what was to unfold. After eight months, the ordeal stopped, but the damage to her development did not go away. We wondered what the future held for us. The Scripture in 1 Corinthians 1:26-29 grabbed my attention as

I realized that many in the world might look at Kimberley as "weak," "low and despised," or "as things that are not."

Following the story of the birth of Jesus and the visit of the shepherds to the manger, Scripture includes one special verse: *But Mary kept all these things and pondered them in her heart* (Luke 2:19 KJV). I have often wondered exactly what this meant. The longer I lived with Kimberley, the more I knew that Mary lived a life where the fire was a friend. Being the mother of our Lord was filled with many Divine and spectacular occasions, but Mary's life was also filled with many tragedies and disappointments. She treasured the special moments to help her get through the hard ones.

I held on to many memories through the years, *pondering them in my heart*. We spent Christmas in Houston with my two siblings and their families in 1985. Bev and Jim had a commitment to go to a New Year's Eve party, so Mother and I were excited to have time with their four children and Kimberley. When we sat down to dinner, I asked who would like to say the blessing. Kimberley raised her hand and shouted, "Me!" We were surprised, as she had only begun to speak six months earlier and had never prayed out loud before, much less put words together in a sentence. We all bowed our heads and waited. She closed her eyes, folded her hands, and prayed, "Thanks food to eat. Bye." Mother, Lindsay, Stewart, Aaron, and Micah all looked at me with big smiles on their faces and burst into happy tears. Kimberley grinned from ear to ear. Like her first word, *hallelujah,* Kimberley's first sentence was to give glory to God! Throughout her life, her favorite word remained *hallelujah,* and her favorite thing to do was to pray.

We loved being with our Texas family. Uncle Jim made Kimberley feel special because he was able to see beyond her physical disabilities into the amazing mind the Lord had given her. People with disabilities need to be surrounded by people who will focus on their strengths rather than on their disabilities. He would sit with her for long periods of time, not saying a word but making her feel special.

Another treasure happened when Kimberley was ten and we discovered that she had no left hip socket, so her left leg was not connected to her pelvis. Following major surgery to create a hip socket and attach the leg to it, she wore a hot pink body cast for several months. One day shortly after the cast was removed, we were at physical therapy. Her therapist shared she had been at a party where Kimberley's brilliant and favorite surgeon, Dr. Lyon, had been. Kimberley asked what she thought of him. The therapist replied that he hadn't said much, so she didn't know. Kimberley's reply was priceless. "That's true, he's taciturn." The therapist looked confused and asked what that meant, and Kimberley replied, "A man of few words." The following month, the school system removed the label *mentally retarded* from her file, saying, "Kimberley appears to be a bright young girl, limited only by her physical impairment."

The following month, the school system removed the label "mentally retarded" from her file.

These little memories sustained me through many experiences that weren't so pleasant. In public school, children with disabilities were kept in a different wing of the school in special classrooms away from children without disabilities. This gave the impression that there was something so different about those children that regular education students shouldn't interact with them. God doesn't feel this way, as evidenced by the Scripture below.

*But God chose what is **foolish** in the world to shame the wise; God chose what is **weak** in the world to shame* *the strong; God chose what is* ***low*** *and* ***despised*** *in the world, even* ***things that are not****, to bring to nothing things that are, so that no human being might boast in the presence of God.* (1 Corinthians 1:26-29 ESV)

Unfortunately, people with disabilities don't get to live in the presence of God only; they live in a world of imperfect people and frequently experience being ignored or rejected by others.

Her Aunt Nancy expressed this beautifully. Kimberley said, "I love you" frequently and expected a response of "I love you, too." This could be annoying to those who didn't understand how her brain worked. Nancy expressed that she learned about the unrelenting love of the Lord by seeing how Kimberley kept after people, showing them love in spite of their not responding to her the way she needed.

We didn't realize what specific disabilities Kimberley had; it took years to get them properly diagnosed. We did know that her language was limited to a few words, and she couldn't walk or crawl. Being physically impaired qualified her for special education. Kimberley entered the three-year-old program at the United Cerebral Palsy School for children with various disabilities when we moved to Tallahassee. Attending three hours a day, two days a week, resulted in solid mental and physical gains as she interacted with children with different disabilities on a regular basis.

Often people have preconceived notions about what is wrong with children with disabilities based on their interactions with what the world calls "normal children." This was true with Kimberley. For example, when she was three, we went to a Christian conference with some well-known presenters. During the meeting, Kimberley started making noises and talking out loud, being a little disruptive. To keep her noises from bothering others, we left the session and stood outside until the teaching was over. During the social hour that followed, the presenter came to me to tell me I was going to have major discipline problems with my daughter if I didn't take authority over her misbehavior while she was young.

I had disciplined Kimberley in every acceptable way I knew. I prayed and spoke Scripture over her. Nothing worked to keep her from talking at times that were socially unacceptable. She seemed compelled to talk, no matter what I did. I sought the Lord and searched Scripture to discover why we didn't have victory in this area.

Ministering healing seemed to be my main call since I studied it constantly to discover solutions for Kimberley. I ministered healing to many people who were touched by the Lord with healing miracles. As a teacher, it was my joy to head up the healing team at Christian Heritage Church. In February 1986, I took a team of people from our church to a two-day Charles and Frances Hunter Healing Explosion in Jacksonville, Florida. At the Victory Breakfast following the healing explosion, I sat at a table with Beverly Lawyer and Darlene McRoberts, who were editing a book on children with disabilities. They invited me to write Kimberley's story for inclusion in their book, *Victorious Survivors*.[1]

Several years after this book was published, I received a call from a mother in south Florida who had read my chapter. She wanted to share some of the lessons she had learned over the years with her daughter. For three hours, we talked and cried together. She was the first person in ten years, outside my family, who understood what we were living through. She described Kimberley and was accurate in every point, even though she had never met her.

She was the first person in ten years, outside my family, who understood what we were living through.

She told me my daughter most likely had something called *sensory defensiveness*. This meant that the senses took in too much information and literally caused pain that could be measured on a scale from low to moderate to severe. I was overwhelmed with this information because it meant Kimberley had been living with pain all these years, even though the teething pain was gone. She suggested that I call Sandra Wainman, an occupational therapist in Orlando, Florida, for an evaluation.

The next morning, I called Sandy Wainman to make an appointment; however, she couldn't see us until January, another two months away. I begged her to work us in if she had an opening. Sensing our need, she assured me that she rarely had cancellations, but she promised to call if an opening occurred. I pleaded with the Lord to open an earlier appointment. The next day, Sandy called to say, "I never have cancellations, but I just had one for Monday morning. Can you be here at 9 a.m. on Monday?" Mother, Kimberley, and I were heading to Texas for my brother David's wedding to a precious woman, Nancy, on Tuesday, so we happily made a four-hour detour south to Orlando on Sunday afternoon.

What a life-changing experience that was! Sandy evaluated Kimberley and confirmed that Kimberley was severely defensive in all her senses. She introduced me to the Wilbarger Protocol. I was to add pressure to Kimberley's sensory diet and use a specific surgical scrub brush and deep pressure massage on her every two hours except when she was sleeping. After the first brushing session, Kimberley's face changed from one of pain and tension to one of peace.

During the evaluation, Kimberley pushed a table over, something for which she was frequently disciplined. Sandy explained to Kimberley that this behavior was "smart problem solving" because her body needed gravity when she was on sensory overload. When she turned over tables, she was helping her brain reorganize from a stressful environment caused by her senses being over stimulated. Kimberley broke out in tears and said, "You mean I'm not a bad person?" My heart broke as I realized that I had been disciplining her for behaviors she couldn't stop and for behaviors her brain needed.

Sandy explained to Kimberley that there were better ways to relieve stress and help her brain reorganize. She taught her to put her hands together with her fingers entwined and pointing upward, with the palms of her hands together, her elbows pointed out away from her body, and to push hard to a slow count of ten. You could see the amazing results in her face and body as she relaxed. This became a tool she used the rest of her life, and her need to turn over tables went away.

I wore a timer set at ninety minutes. When it went off, I "brushed" Kimberley and gave her a pressure massage. Sandra recommended we do this for two weeks to see what results we would obtain. The outcome was so dramatic for Kimberley, I continued to brush her for four months.

Kimberley pulled herself around using a soldier crawl for ten years. She had not been able to get up on all fours and crawl, much less walk. After only two weeks of this new protocol, Mother and I were in the living room watching Kimberley while we talked. Suddenly Kimberley said, "Mommy, watch!" She pushed up on her hands and knees and started to crawl. This was a miracle! We praised the Lord for getting us that appointment with Sandra Wainman so we could learn about sensory defensiveness.

We saw many other improvements. Kimberley was able to use a spoon to feed herself. She could hold a pencil and use enough pressure to make marks on paper. She wrote her first word, *Carol,* the name of a dear friend. She could dial the telephone and "talk" to friends. She loved to play Tetris and quickly went from three lines to one hundred lines. Best of all, she started looking me in the eye.

I will never forget the moment she took my face in her hands, looked deep into my eyes, and said, "Mommy, you are so beautiful!"

A few months later, another occupational therapist, Patricia Wilbarger, was holding a workshop in Atlanta, Georgia on sensory defensiveness. This was the same person who developed the Wilbarger Protocol that had turned around many areas of Kimberley's life. I quickly registered for the three-day seminar.

During one of the breaks on the first morning of the seminar, I stood in line to meet this amazing woman who had profoundly changed our lives. I wanted to thank her and share some of the positive benefits we had received from her Wilbarger Protocol. Pat was thrilled with all she heard about Kimberley. Throughout the week we talked as often as possible. At the end of the workshop, she told me she was doing another workshop in Tallahassee for teachers the following month and invited me to be her guest. She indicated she wanted to meet Kimberley and asked if she could stay in our home

I stood in line to meet this amazing woman who had profoundly changed our lives.

during her week in Tallahassee. For one week, I had the privilege of becoming friends with and learning all I could from Pat Wilbarger. During that week, she certified me to teach her protocol.

Doors opened for me to teach one to ten-hour workshops for parents and teachers dealing with sensory disabilities in their homes and classrooms. We saw dramatic growth in children with ADHD and those on the autistic spectrum. It was apparent that what the Lord had done for Kimberley, I was to share with others. What joy!

I realized that I had let the opinion of others influence the way I handled my daughter, particularly in difficult areas. As with her impulse to push tables over, Kimberley could not help yelling out at inappropriate times. Although I hadn't understood why she was doing this, I knew it wasn't misbehavior.

Children display misbehavior and inappropriate behavior. These are two enormously different things, although they can look exactly alike. Misbehavior takes place when a child intentionally disobeys or does something on purpose they know is wrong. Inappropriate behaviors take place when children do something they may or may not know is wrong, but they can't stop themselves from the behavior. Misbehavior needs to be disciplined.

Inappropriate behavior needs to have logical consequences that help the child learn that there are consequences for their behavior. Turning over tables and yelling out were inappropriate, but they were not misbehavior.

One of the most difficult things parents must do is to discern what is causing unacceptable behavior in their children. Is it misbehavior or inappropriate behavior? This had been a challenge because people would tell me Kimberley's behavior was wrong and I needed to discipline her, when I knew discipline wouldn't work. When I disciplined her for inappropriate behavior, it negatively reinforced the behavior and caused it to increase. What a conundrum!

The Lord provided an answer through Pat Wilbarger. The sense that was most compromised in Kimberley was her auditory sense. Her hearing was so sensitive that she lived in pain. When we were at church and the music stopped, she could not handle the shift from loud music to quiet talking or preaching. Her hyperacute hearing was so stimulated that she had to speak to diminish the intense pain caused by the music.

Music spoke to her soul. She had listened to worship and praise music in her room twenty-four hours a day, seven days a week since she was a baby. She kept her music so quiet that I could barely hear it, but it kept her peaceful and stopped other distractions. The Wilbarger Protocol helped reduce all of Kimberley's senses from severe to moderate, except the auditory sense which remained in the severe range.

Pat suggested we go to Developmental Therapy Associates (DTA) in Durham, North Carolina. They specialized in Auditory Integration Therapy (AIT),[2] a treatment developed by a French doctor, Guy Berard.[3] AIT was introduced in America by Annabel Stehli's powerful book, *The Sound of a Miracle.*[4] Annabel's daughter Georgiana went from being labeled severely autistic and functionally retarded to gifted after the sensory integration of AIT.

We went to North Carolina for a ten-day treatment that consisted of two thirty-minute sessions each day, one in the morning and one in the afternoon, during which Kimberley received occupational and physical therapy. The results were remarkable.

At the beginning of her treatment, Kimberley measured off the pain grid when the volume of sound was above 50-55 decibels. The sounds that pushed her all the way off the pain grid were *T-K-S-Sh*. Laughing, the staff asked me if Kimberley ever responded to me when I said her name harshly, particularly when I was disciplining her. I thought of the times I said "**K**imberley **Sh**epard ...!" She never responded. They explained that she was not being defiant. Rather, her brain shut down to defend itself against the level of pain produced by *K* and *Sh* sounds in her name. She did not even hear what I was saying. I went through more self-condemnation, even though there was no way I could have known the sound of her name produced pain!

This meant that even in our peaceful home with soft to moderate sounds, she could be sensory overloaded, particularly when there was too much talking. I had learned that I could not read to her more than a few minutes before she would try to tear the book. When I did try to read to her, she had little retention of what was read. If I went into the living room and pretended that I was reading out loud to myself while she played in her room, she would remember everything I read.

By the end of ten days of treatment, Kimberley was a different child. Her balance improved, allowing her to crawl better and sit more easily in a chair. She spent the afternoon pulling herself from one bed to the other in our hotel room, something that would have been impossible for her earlier in the week. Her speech was clearer, and she was able to make many new sounds. Best of all, she could tolerate sounds up to 75-80 decibels, like the noise of a washing machine, for short periods of time. This dramatically changed her life; although when she moved from loud to quiet environments, her need to talk to drown out the pain of hearing never went away.

The precious staff at DTA, Sandra Wainman, and Pat Wilbarger are heroes of mine. Each helped us move to a new level of independence and discovery. We pray blessings for these ladies and know the Lord smiles down on them. *Truly, I say to you, as you did it to one of the least of these my brothers, you did it to me* (Matthew 25:40 ESV).

One of the reasons I have gone to lengths in this chapter to describe the impact of sensory issues for Kimberley is that most people on the autistic spectrum have some form of sensory defensiveness. This turned out to be the number one disability with which we contended. Sensory defensiveness can affect people with learning disabilities, Attention Deficit Disorders (ADD/ADHD), Obsessive Compulsive Disorder (OCD), Asperger's Syndrome, Pervasive Developmental Disorders-Not Otherwise Specified (PDD-NOS), Specific Learning Disabilities (SLD) and many others. While there are many strategies that can help people who are sensory defensive, these individuals are often misunderstood. The situation is exacerbated by the judgment and condemnation of others, rather than compassion and understanding.

Judgment can come from well-meaning people. One Sunday morning a mother and daughter came into the bathroom at Christian Heritage, having no idea I was in there. Kimberley was facing surgery, and I had asked for prayer. The mother's words pierced my heart as she spoke to her daughter: "I wonder what is wrong with Mary-Friend's faith that Kimberley hasn't been healed?" They proceeded to talk about me, wondering how I could lead the healing team when Kimberley had not been healed. I was devastated and remained in my stall until I knew they were gone. I wondered if others felt the same way.

Not only are children with disabilities judged by others, so are their parents. These two ladies reminded me of Job's friends who are known for their betrayal of Job when he became covered with boils and lost everything of importance to him. While Job's friends did evidence friendship by coming to visit and mourn with him initially, after a short period of time, they each expounded about the reasons God allows people to suffer. They assumed that Job was suffering because he had done something wrong, rather than wondering what God's plan was for Job through the fire in which he was living.

I was reminded of the question one of the disciples asked Jesus when they saw a man who had been blind since birth. This was what I felt as I heard that mother talking.

As he passed by, he saw a man blind from birth. And his disciples asked him, "Rabbi, who sinned, this man or his parents, that he was born blind?" Jesus answered, "It was not that this man sinned, or his parents, but that the works of God might be displayed in him. (John 9:1-3 ESV)

That afternoon I had a conversation with the Lord to ask if I was demonstrating a lack of faith by allowing Kimberley to go through surgery. "Job's friends" had not come directly to me with their concern about and condemnation of my faith, but what I heard from them deeply influenced what I was feeling. The Lord asked me a question and the ensuing conversation was just what I needed.

"MaryFriend, who wrote the book of Acts?"

Luke.

"What was Luke?"

A doctor.

"Why do you think I had a medical doctor write My Holy Ghost book of the Bible?"

Relief flooded me. Doctors can be God's tools. Holy Spirit reached down into my heart and erased all the condemnation and confusion I was feeling. A deep assurance filled me that our Lord was orchestrating our lives.

We had seen many miracles in Kimberley's life. The Lord had healed her at different times. What He was telling me in this conversation was that there would be times He used medical doctors to take care of a medical issue. I was at peace that she should go through surgery this time because I was assured that *the power of God* was *at work in* Kimberley. This scripture assured me further: *For I consider that the sufferings of this present time are not worth comparing with the glory that is to be revealed to us* (Romans 8:18 ESV). I knew we could face anything the Lord allowed us to walk through.

Chapter 8

Demolishing Strongholds

The weapons we use to wage war are not worldly. On the contrary, they have God's power for demolishing strongholds.

2 Corinthians 10:4 CJB

STRONGHOLDS HAD little meaning to me before Kimberley came into my life. I often looked at this verse wondering why God gave me the power to demolish strongholds, especially since I didn't really know what they were or why I would want to demolish them. I was content to live with the baggage I had, thinking it was who I was. When the Lord raises my curiosity about a Scripture like 2 Corinthians 10:4, it is typically a sign He is about to teach me a lesson.

To understand what a spiritual stronghold is, I had to learn what physical strongholds are. The best image I could find was of a fortress with solid, thick walls and a deep, wide moat around it. To conquer a fortified fortress requires that the strongholds be demolished and torn down before the ground can be taken. Strongholds were built defensively to protect what lived in the fortress from being conquered.

What would you want to know if you were going to war against an army that was surrounded by a solid stronghold? Why is it necessary to know about the strongholds of your enemies? Why would the best generals examine both the commander of the enemy as well as his subordinate officers before engaging in war with them? In any battle, it is essential to know the vulnerabilities of your enemies as well as their strengths.

I am the enemy of Lucifer, who hates those of us who are children of God. Lucifer is actively trying to build strongholds in our hearts to give his demons a place to safely live untouched by God. As children of God who want to live in freedom, we need to know what these strongholds are, who is living in them, and how to eliminate them from our lives.

Matthew 12:29 and Mark 2:27 make it clear that the only way an enemy can attack a fortress is to *tie up the strongman first*. That is our job—to bind or tie up the strongman first. Then we are free to *ransack the house and take his possessions* away from him. We are free to take back the land the enemy has taken from us where he has been hiding in a stronghold in our hearts. Until we apply this knowledge, Lucifer continues to attack us in our most vulnerable areas, so the strongholds that give him permission to live in our hearts are enlarged. His goal is to keep the love of God out of the areas of our heart where he has strongholds.

Spiritual strongholds are walls we build up when something has a strong hold on us that keeps us in bondage. We build strongholds to protect ourselves from pain or from things that may harm us. The enemy knows where our weaknesses are because he has been working to produce them since we were in our mother's womb. God created a Kingdom purpose for each of us before the foundation of the world (Psalm 139:16). Satan devised a plot and plan to keep us from our Kingdom purpose. He is waging a battle to keep us from meeting our Kingdom purpose on earth.

We build strongholds to protect ourselves from pain or from things that may harm us.

Ephesians 6:12 clearly tells us that *we are not struggling against human beings, but against the rulers, authorities and cosmic powers governing this darkness, against the spiritual forces of evil in the heavenly realm* (CJB). Every time I look at the struggles I have had in my life, I can see they go back to the demonic forces that attacked either me or my daughter. I learned to ask what spiritual forces of evil were keeping me in pain or bringing harm to one of us.

How do strongholds form in our heart?

Hurts from people we trust can be devastating. Kimberley was attacked by a spirit of rejection when she was most vulnerable. While she was in my womb, her father begged that she be aborted. At thirteen months she was in the hospital for twenty-eight days, where she almost died multiple times. Each day was a struggle to keep her alive. The chaplain of the hospital was sent to counsel me to let her die. When she was eighteen months old, her father divorced me and walked out of our lives completely.

How did these actions build a stronghold? On the first occasion when rejection takes place, a person's emotions say, "Ouch, that hurt. I don't want that to happen again!" They build a tiny wall around that part of their heart for protection. The enemy smiles. He knows he hit a raw nerve, so he attacks that spot again and again using the same spirits. Each time rejection occurred for Kimberley, the wall thickened until her heart and emotions were sealed from that pain. Unfortunately, when a person seals a part of their heart from pain, they are building a stronghold that also seals it from the love of the Lord.

To destroy a stronghold, one needs to know what the stronghold is and what spirits are in the stronghold. In Kimberley's case, the spirits of rejection and betrayal were huge! In the next chapter, I will share how she was delivered from this demon.

What is exciting is that we have the authority and power to demolish strongholds! *The weapons we use to wage war are not worldly. On the contrary, they have God's power for demolishing strongholds* (2 Corinthians 10:4 CJB). The blood of the Lamb, our testimony, and loving God more than life are three key weapons we have against satan (Revelation 12:11). Declarations we make based on the Word of God are another powerful weapon. This was the weapon Jesus used when satan tried to tempt Him and He replied, *"It is written."*

At the center of every stronghold is a broken heart.

Do you ever feel irritated, angry, depressed, despondent, hopeless, forsaken, or devastated? *We have all kinds of troubles, but we are not crushed; we are perplexed, yet not in despair; persecuted, yet not abandoned; knocked down, yet not destroyed* (2 Corinthians 4:8-9 CJB). The Lord never wanted us to be this way, so He has a plan to overcome the trauma we have experienced, inflicted by ourselves or by others, often when we were children.

Stop thinking about what others did to you. Assume responsibility for your reactions to their negative behavior. Assume responsibility for the judgments you made of the people who hurt you. We can't help the sin in others, but we are responsible for the way we react to it. When I take hurt from another person, I ask myself why that hurt me. The Lord always shows me a place in my own heart that He wants to heal.

When we don't see ourselves the way the Lord sees us, ... we are saying we are ashamed of the person the Lord intended us to be.

For the mouth speaks what overflows from the heart (Matthew 12:34 CJB). When we don't see ourselves the way the Lord sees us, we speak negative things about ourselves; we see ourselves as less than God made us to be. We are saying we are ashamed of the person the Lord intended us to be. Can you think of things you say about yourself that don't line up with what God says about you?

Being a member of the deliverance team at Christian Heritage in Tallahassee taught me much about deliverance. I watched people go through deliverance and become totally free. It was exhilarating! In several months, however, some were back in the bondages they had prior to deliverance. I asked the Lord why they couldn't keep their freedom. Boldly, I told the Lord I didn't want to take anyone else through deliverance until I learned how to help them remain free.

The key is pulling down strongholds!

Deliverance cleans the house, but if one goes through deliverance without tearing down the stronghold (house) where the demons lived, the demons have permission to return to their house. Not only do they return, but they bring seven friends with them making them eight times stronger.

> *"When the unclean spirit has gone out of a person, it passes through waterless places seeking rest, but finds none. Then it says, 'I will return to my house from which I came.' And when it comes, it finds the house empty, swept, and put in order. Then it goes and brings with it seven other spirits more evil than itself, and they enter and dwell there, and the last state of that person is worse*

than the first. So also will it be with this evil generation."

(Matthew 12:43-45 ESV)

This passage caught my attention, and I determined I would learn how to tear down and demolish strongholds before I took another person through deliverance.

Deliverance ministers often ask a person to give a history of the traumas and experiences of their life. From this information, Holy Spirit reveals what needs to be addressed during the deliverance session. This seemed invasive and cumbersome to me. I asked Holy Spirit if that was necessary for healing. Revelation on this question came from a surprising source.

Dr. Wilder Penfield, neurosurgeon and devout Christian, provided insight into demolishing strongholds, even though he never addressed this subject. By mapping the brain through mild electrical shock, he discovered that people have memory about their lives stored in their brains even after the ability to consciously recall the events ends. He developed a surgical procedure where he was able to open a person's brain but keep the person awake so they could converse during the surgery. Through this he learned that he could stimulate the temporal lobes in the brain and cause people to have memories that were so lifelike and credible it was as if they were happening to the person in the present. The brain remembers everything, and everything can be retrieved instantly.[1]

Holy Spirit is better than Dr. Penfield's procedure. He is a gentleman and can selectively bring up those experiences from our past that He knows we need to deal with, because He wants us to live victorious lives. My prayer and ministry partner, Jim, and I came up with a strategy for demolishing strongholds based on this principle. We developed our strategy using my personal experience.

Holy Spirit ... can selectively bring up those experiences from our past that He knows we need to deal with.

My Story of Freedom from Bondage

One fellow I dated in Tallahassee asked me why I expected him to reject me. I had no idea what he was talking about. He wanted to know why I wouldn't let people know who I really am. I kept three areas of my life private when I first met someone: that I was divorced, that my daughter had multiple disabilities, and that I had a PhD. These were areas that had caused me to be rejected, so I kept them private until I trusted the friendship.

When my friend asked me why I expected to be rejected, I had no answer for him. He encouraged me to ask Holy Spirit and see what He told me. After my friend left, I lay on the couch to be alone with Holy Spirit.

After about fifteen minutes, Holy Spirit took me to a time I was in the first grade. It was a dark, stormy day. As I sat on the water fountain on the school porch, I was surrounded by all the other first graders waiting on our mothers to pick us up from school. My sister and I rode our bikes to school since we only lived a few blocks away. I remember thinking, "My mom isn't going to pick me up. She has meetings at the church and is too busy." Then I saw her car turning the corner in line with all the other mothers. At that point, I ran out in the rain, jumped on my bike, and rode home.

My action baffled me. I had not thought about this event since the day it happened, yet I remembered this experience as if it happened yesterday. Holy Spirit didn't need to take me through all the times I experienced rejection during my life. He took me to one of two key events that showed where the expectation of rejection took root in my life.

Questions flooded my mind. Why would I do such a thing? Why would Holy Spirit show me this scene when I was asking about men? He skipped right over my divorce. Holy Spirit gently told me "Don't you see? When you were six years old you expected your mother not to pick you up after school on a rainy day. But she did."

Why would Holy Spirit show me this scene when I was asking about men?

Three weeks later, Kimberley and I were in Miami where I was teaching a two-week in-service class for the teachers at one of the elementary schools. Kimberley went to sleep early, so I had time in our hotel room to read and talk with the Lord. I asked Holy Spirit why He showed me the rainy-day adventure.

Rather than answering me, He took me to a time in my life I didn't consciously remember. During the first few months of my life, I had a severe milk intolerance that resulted in many digestive problems. I cried much of the day and night for two months. My parents tried everything—goat milk, cow milk, anything they could find.

Holy Spirit showed me a night during this time when I could not be comforted. My mother in frustration snapped at my daddy. This was extremely unusual because Mother was a calm and controlled lady. She was deeply bothered by her reaction to my crying. From that point forward, Daddy walked the floor with me, and Mother took care of Beverley, who was two years older than I. This seemed to solve the problem. When they discovered I could digest buttermilk easily, I was satisfied, and my crying stopped.

I bonded with my daddy as he cared for me, but baby MaryFriend had taken rejection from my mother not taking care of me for most of that time. Mother was extremely loving toward me, but I had missed a key bonding time between mother and daughter during those two months. This resulted in my building a stronghold to protect my heart against the pain of the expectation of rejection from those I loved.

Using the five-step prayer process with Holy Spirit, any Spirit-led person can demolish strongholds.

Using the following five-step prayer process with Holy Spirit, any Spirit-led person can demolish strongholds.

1) Identify the hurt.

First, identify the hurt and ask Holy Spirit to show you where it entered and took root in your life. In my case, I asked why I expected men to reject me. The identification of the hurt is our responsibility. What can hurt you? What kind of situations cause you to say, "Ouch, that hurt" or "That makes me angry" or something similar? Write them down and take them one at a time through the following steps so you can obtain freedom.

2) Receive and extend forgiveness.

Second, receive forgiveness and extend forgiveness. Scripture tells us that our heavenly Father will forgive us because we have forgiven others.

> *Forgive us what we have done wrong, as we too have forgiven those who have wronged us. ... For if you forgive others their offenses, your heavenly Father will also forgive you; but if you do not forgive others their offenses, your heavenly Father will not forgive yours.* (Matthew 6:12, 14-15 CJB)

Forgiveness is not an option for a Christian. Forgiveness is a command of God, and we must do it if we want His forgiveness when we do wrong.

I asked whom I needed to forgive. The first person I forgave was my mother for not being there when I needed her. She had done nothing wrong, but as a baby I perceived her actions as rejection. In reality, she needed rest and distraction from my crying. I forgave my daddy for taking my mother's place. I forgave myself for causing all this ruckus with my milk intolerance. I forgave God for not taking care of the situation when He could have stopped it.

Sometimes we have unforgiveness that is legitimate, but other times we have irrational thoughts. Sometimes we hold something against a person when they haven't done anything wrong. Sometimes we hold God responsible for not acting on our behalf on *our* timetable. Unforgiveness is a strange phenomenon that must be dealt with because it holds us in bondage.

Unforgiveness ... holds us in bondage.

The Lord promises that He will forgive our wickedness and will remember our sin no more (Jeremiah 31:34). Does this mean God forgets our sins? Forgiveness doesn't mean you forget what was done to you. When our heavenly Father forgives us, He chooses not to remember. He chooses not to hold our sins against us. He chooses not to ever use our sins as a weapon against us. Two more times He says He will remember our sins no more!

> *Because I will be merciful toward their wickednesses and remember their sins no more.* (Hebrews 8:12 CJB)

And their sins and their wickednesses I will remember no more. (Hebrews 10:17 CJB)

When you forgive, you are saying that you will follow the example of the Father and *will* not to remember offenses committed against you. That means you may recall what happened and even use it in a teachable moment, but you choose never again to use that offense against the person who inflicted it. Forgiveness means you *choose* not to remember. As an act of your will, you will not bring up or use what has been forgiven against a person. You are setting that person free, and as you do, you set yourself free.

You are setting that person free, and as you do, you set yourself free.

3) Demolish the strongholds.

Third, stronghold destruction and demolition must take place. The stronghold was a thick wall around a place in my heart that housed the demons that harassed me regarding the expectation of rejection. I asked Holy Spirit to send a Holy Ghost wall buster to blast every brick that was a part of that stronghold. Demolishing the fortifications means no demon can stay there. Tearing down the wall of the stronghold means the demons have no place to return.

> *For although we do live in the world, we do not wage war in a worldly way; because the weapons we use to wage war are not worldly. On the contrary, they have God's power for demolishing strongholds. We demolish arguments and every arrogance that raises itself up against the knowledge of God; we take every thought captive and make it obey the Messiah.* (2 Corinthians 10:3-5 CJB)

Scripture tells us we have God's power to demolish strongholds.

4) Experience deliverance.

Fourth, deliverance is necessary after the stronghold has been demolished. Two options exist: you can take yourself through self-deliverance or you can ask for help from several deliverance ministers. Some of the last words of Jesus written in Mark 16:15-18 tell us to share the Good News with everyone. He then tells us that signs will follow those who believe in Jesus and who believe in His name. We are told we can lay

Deliverance is necessary after the stronghold has been demolished.

hands on the sick and they will recover and that we can drive out demons.

In this situation, I chose to take myself through self-deliverance from the spirit of expectation of rejection, among others. I was ready to take back the land the enemy had held from me. I was ready to possess the land of my heart!

5) Heal the brokenhearted.

Fifth, broken hearts need to be healed. Psalm 147:3 says the Lord *heals the brokenhearted and binds up their wounds* (CJB). Jesus proclaims:

> *The Spirit of the Lord is upon me, because he hath anointed me to preach the gospel to the poor; he hath sent me to heal the brokenhearted, to preach deliverance to the captives, and recovering of sight to the blind, to set at liberty them that are bruised.* (Luke 4:18 KJV)

What a powerful ministry our Lord had! This was exactly what I needed to walk free.

The word *brokenhearted* in this passage is the Greek word *suntribo* that means *to crush completely, to break in pieces, or to bruise.*[2] *Deliverance* is the Greek word *aphesis* that means *to pardon, forgiveness, liberty, and freedom.*[3] What perfect words to describe what deliverance does in us when we are released from captivity through the demolition of strongholds! The Lord wants to take our crushed spirits and broken hearts and heal them completely through His forgiveness.

I prayed a simple prayer. "Lord, heal baby MaryFriend from the pain of rejection that came into her when she was a tiny baby—her perceived rejection from her mother. Set her free from the expectation of rejection and heal her broken heart."

I made the decision to choose not to focus on what had held me in bondage and to march forward in righteousness and holiness. I had to *remember not the former things, nor consider the things of old* (Isaiah 43:18 ESV). It was time to let my spirit and mind be renewed by Holy Spirit so I could be clothed in this new nature the Lord was giving to me. It was time to embrace the truth and to believe what God said about me (Ephesians 4:23-24).

The Lord promised to give me a new heart and put a new spirit inside me; He promised to take the stony heart out of my flesh and give me a heart of flesh (Ezekiel 36:26). In one evening alone with Holy Spirit, I gained freedom!

Mother, Kimberley, and I lived together in Tallahassee from 1985-95. Every night when I was ready to go to bed, I would go to Mother's room, chat a little, and then kiss her good night. Mother was not much of a toucher or a hugger, except with Kimberley. When Kimberley and I returned from Miami after this experience of demolishing strongholds, my mother came into my room and kissed me good night for the first time in our adult lives. *She* was free and *I* was free. She had no knowledge of what had happened to me, but she was free, too. POWERFUL!

Take your heart and ask the Lord to show you one area on which He wants you to work. What makes you hurt, angry, irritated? Then let the Holy Spirit lead you through these steps to freedom. Take back the land that the enemy has stolen from you.

Chapter 9

He Set the Captives Free

God anointed Jesus of Nazareth with the Holy Spirit and with power. He went about doing good and healing all who were oppressed by the devil, for God was with him.

Acts 10:38 ESV

WHEN THE LORD CALLED me to a ministry that included healing, I was excited to be involved in this aspect of the ministry of Jesus. I knew that Jesus said, *Truly, truly, I say to you, whoever believes in me will also do the works that I do; and greater works than these will he do, because I am going to the Father* (John 14:12 ESV). I was able to minister healing to many people and saw amazing healings.

When I started ministering healing, I had a conversation with the Lord about the second part of Acts 10:38. What a gracious and tolerant God we serve! It was clear to me from Acts 10:38 that disease often comes from the devil. I told the Lord I was excited and willing to minister healing, but I didn't want anything to do with demons. Stories of people who were possessed or oppressed by the devil filled my head, and I didn't want that to be a part of my life or ministry. I really didn't believe that Christians could have demons, so since I was mostly ministering to Christians, this part of the Scripture could be done by someone else!

During our two years in Colorado, the Lord had put me in my own Bible school in the Lighthouse Christian Bookstore, where I could immerse myself in books and tapes about Holy Spirit and healing. When He moved us to Tallahassee in 1995, the Lord began to show me what Holy Spirit could do through an ordinary woman and a child clothed with His Divine love and power.

Through the ministry of Charles and Frances Hunter, I acquired a boldness to reach out to others who are sick and hurting. As a member of a healing team at many of their Healing Explosions, I saw what the Lord could do through His servants. At the Jacksonville Healing Explosion, I had the privilege of participating with a large group of believers to see a leg that had been amputated six inches above the knee grow back. When I ministered to the gentleman, his leg was several inches below the knee, and it had transformed to look just like the other leg, tanned and with hair. I felt the pulsation of the leg as it slowly grew out, although I didn't see the conclusion of the miracle which continued to take place throughout the night. During that service, I was healed of neck pain I had suffered for twenty years. Receiving His marvelous healing and seeing it flow through me to others was overwhelming!

The Lord left me alone for about six months and let me experience the euphoria of seeing people healed in the name of Jesus by the *dunamis* power of Holy Spirit. On Sunday nights after church, many of the singles went out for coffee and fellowship. One Sunday night after most had left, my friend Jim and I stood in the parking lot talking with another friend, Rachel (not her real name). She shared how she had been raised in a family that practiced Silva Mind Control and the negative effect it had on her. As she shared, Rachel started manifesting self-mutilating behaviors that could only be demonic. Jim and I had no idea what to do, but we couldn't let her hurt herself or run out into the street.

We did what we now know is not recommended by most deliverance ministers. We encircled her with our arms. I was in front, and Jim was behind her. Jim started pleading the blood of Jesus over her, and I said the name of Jesus over and over. We had no idea what to do, so we used the only tools we had—the precious Blood and Name of Jesus. The blood saves and redeems us from the curse of the law; the blood cleanses and sanctified us. We are told to believe in the name of Jesus and that its power will heal the sick and cast out demons. Slowly, she calmed down, and this event passed.

I was overwhelmed to see what a destructive enemy the devil could be. I was more overwhelmed to know that I felt completely powerless to help Rachel should another similar situation happen to her. The devil is ready to pull us down if we let him, and the enemy was ready to fill me with fear after the parking lot encounter. Psalm 34:4 says, *I sought the LORD, and he answered me; he delivered me from all my fears* (KJV).

I was overwhelmed to see what a destructive enemy the devil could be.

I sought the Lord only to learn He was about to move me to another level of commitment after that night. Something I quickly learned was that the enemy showed up every time I made spiritual leaps in my relationship with the Lord. The enemy would often attack me in my most vulnerable place, my daughter. Kimberley started mutilating herself. She would gouge her eyes until they bled. I was completely undone by this but had no idea what I was supposed to do.

The Lord led me to ten days of prayer and fasting, seeking answers to Kimberley's destructive behavior. Over the next ten days, He opened my eyes to deliverance in multiple, remarkable ways, and I realized dealing with the oppression of the devil was not going to be an option I could deny.

I realized dealing with the oppression of the devil was not going to be an option I could deny.

It had begun with Rachel in the parking lot and now it was manifesting in new unacceptable behaviors in Kimberley. During my fast, I heard Holy Spirit tell me that Kimberley needed to go through deliverance and that Frank would take her through. I was dating a fellow named Frank at the time, so I assumed I was making this up.

I went out to Christian Heritage where we had an anointed prayer room in which I loved to spend time. As I left my car to enter the building, a gentleman approached me and asked where our deliverance team met. He was there for a session. I had no idea that my church had a deliverance team, much less what a deliverance team did, so I sent him to the office for directions.

That baffled me since Holy Spirit had told me Kimberley needed deliverance. What was the Lord saying to me? Instead of going to the prayer room, I headed to see Bonnie, our church counselor, to inquire about deliverance and our deliverance team. Bonnie was free, so we sat down to chat with a cup of coffee. My questions poured out, and she realized I was completely uninformed when it came to deliverance. She asked if I had read *Pigs in the Parlor* by Frank and Ida Mae Hammond. The look on her face said volumes when I replied that I was unfamiliar with the book.

She realized I was completely uninformed when it came to deliverance.

She gave me a copy of *Pigs in the Parlor: A Practical Guide to Deliverance* and asked that I read it and then we could talk. I went home and started reading a book that was so compelling I couldn't stop reading until I finished it that night. My eyes were opened to some of the blocks I held about demons. On the first page, they explained that Christians cannot be demon-possessed because possession implies that a person is owned by the devil. We are children of God and therefore cannot be possessed by the devil.

> *Or do you not know that your body is a temple of the Holy Spirit within you, whom you have from God? You are not your own, for you were bought with a price. So glorify God in your body.* (1 Corinthians 6:19-20 ESV)

When I thought about all Jesus suffered on the cross to set me free, I knew it included my salvation, healing, and freedom from oppression by the devil.

Oppression, on the other hand, *is* possible for a Christian. The devil hates us and the One we love. If a Christian wants to be free from oppression by the devil, it is possible. The Word tells us, *Submit yourselves therefore to God. Resist the devil, and he will flee from you* (James 4:7 ESV). What a marvelous promise in the Word: submit, resist, and watch the devil flee. The Hammonds wrote that "the authority comes through salvation; the power comes through the baptism in the Holy Spirit."[1]

One additional quote that changed my mind about deliverance was one they cited from Billy Graham:

> *All of us engaged in Christian work are constantly aware of the fact that we have to do battle with supernatural forces and powers. ... It is perfectly obvious to all*

of us in spiritual work that people can be possessed by demons, harassed by them and controlled by them. More and more ministers will have to learn to use the power of God to release people from these terrible possessions by the devil.[2]

Billy Graham used the word *possessed* where I believe the word should be *oppressed* for Christians, but his point struck me as valid.

It was clear to me that the Lord wanted Kimberley taken through deliverance. It was evident that this is a legitimate part of His ministry to His flock. In the back of their book, the Hammonds included three pages of common demon groupings. Demons live in families with a strongman over the group. I wondered which demons might be oppressing Kimberley, since her life had been full of so much trauma.

I finished reading the book in the middle of the night, and Kimberley was sleeping soundly. This book caused a shift in my thinking, and I decided to check it out. I took my flashlight, the book opened to the list of demon groups, and a pencil as I crept into her room. I sat beside her bed, put my hand on her stomach, and started reading the list of demons. Shock and amusement overtook me as I read. At times, Kimberley moved restlessly in her bed. At other times, she yawned or made strange noises. Sometimes she moved my hand from her stomach. Every time she manifested, I put a check mark by the demon grouping that had cause her to react.

As I reviewed the list where she reacted, some were completely obvious: rejection, trauma, death, pain, abortion, among many others. What was I to do with this newfound knowledge? In my ignorance, I decided to choose one of the demons and take her through deliverance as outlined in the book. Rejection seemed the most obvious.

Kimberley had faced rejection when she was in my womb. Her father had begged me to abort her. During her twenty-eight days in the hospital, her father would not visit her and encouraged me to let her die. The chaplain of the hospital counseled me to let her die to save my marriage. The ultimate rejection came when Darrell divorced me, so she never saw her dad again. Rejection seemed like the perfect place to start.

The next morning, Kimberley crawled into my bed to wake me up and cuddle for a while. While holding her in my arms, I picked up the book and read the Deliverance Prayer the Hammonds had borrowed from Derek Prince. The next step the Hammonds recommended was "Taking Authority Over Spiritual Powers." Using the power of binding and loosing, I bound the spirit of rejection and forbade the enemy from operating.

> *I will give you the keys (authority) of the kingdom of heaven; and whatever you bind [forbid, declare to be improper and unlawful] on earth will have [already] been bound in heaven, and whatever you loose [permit, declare lawful] on earth will have [already] been loosed in heaven.* (Matthew 16:19 AMP)

The Lord gave to us the authority of heaven to bind satan and loose his targets from his power! Then I commanded all the spirits of rejection to "unlink themselves from one another."[3]

The final step was to command the demons to go. ... This totally backfired on me.

The final step was to command the demons to go. I read the Hammonds' paragraph verbatim, inserting the name of the spirit of rejection (in brackets below).

> *[Rejection], I know that you are there. I know of your presence and of your evil works. I tell you that you have no right to stay in [Kimberley]. [Kimberley] belongs to Jesus Christ. Jesus purchased [Kimberley] with His own blood. [Her] body is the temple of the Holy Spirit.*

Everything that defiles is cast out. You are a trespasser, and you must go. I command you [spirit of rejection] to go now in the name of Jesus.[4]

This totally backfired on me. Having just celebrated her fourth birthday, Kimberley was tiny, weighing only twenty-one pounds. When I commanded the spirit of rejection to leave her, she stiffened her body, demonstrated supernatural strength so I could hardly hold her, and scratched my back so hard it drew blood.

I was shocked! I mumbled something to the devil about giving up, and Kimberley returned to her normal self. What took place in that short period of time showed me that demons were real! I had lost this battle, but now I knew what was at stake and I promised myself we would not lose the war!

The singles from church were having a beach party that weekend and Bonnie would be there. I was excited to talk to her and another friend, Darlene, about my disastrous adventure into deliverance. They were remarkably compassionate as they taught me that one should have at least one other person to assist during deliverance. In my exuberance, I had completely missed that key point.

Darlene shared that the Hammonds were going to be in Perry, Florida for two days ministering on deliverance and asked if I wanted to go with her and Bonnie. Sunday night, Frank Hammond taught on rejection. God had planned this just for me. During the time of fellowship after their amazing teaching, I shared Kimberley's story briefly with Ida Mae, focusing on my daughter's new self-mutilating behaviors and my uninformed attempt at deliverance.

Ida Mae asked me to wait a moment while she talked to her husband. When she returned, she asked if I could bring Kimberley for deliverance the following day. My mind was spinning as I remembered just one week earlier, the Lord had told me Kimberley needed to go through deliverance and that it would be done by Frank. Who would have believed the Frank would be Frank Hammond, one of the authors of *Pigs in the Parlor*!

Just one week earlier, the Lord had told me Kimberley needed to go through deliverance and that it would be done by Frank.

Darlene drove us to Perry on Monday morning and played with Kimberley while I gave the team an extensive review of her history. Five ministers were in the room: Frank and Ida Mae, their daughter and her husband, and the pastor of the church. While I talked, the pastor took extensive notes on the unholy spirits he discerned were present. After an hour and half of sharing our story from conception to the present, everyone bowed their heads to hear what Holy Spirit had to say.

One by one, they opened their eyes and looked at me. Ida Mae spoke first and said, "We can't take Kimberley through deliverance until you go through first. You need to be a clean vessel to help your daughter remain clean after we finish today." I agreed, and they took me through one of the most amazing experiences ever! I felt like a spiritual virgin when they finished.

Next, it was Kimberley's turn. I held her on my lap and Frank and Ida Mae took her through a gentle deliverance. They never raised their voices but spoke authoritatively to the demon spirits. The others were singing and praying softly in English and in tongues. Kimberley mostly manifested through yawns, coughs, burps, and hiccups.

It was reassuring that the terrifying manifestations I experienced with my first adventure into deliverance were not present. The Hammonds knew their authority in the Lord, and the demons recognized it also. The unwelcome spirits gently marched out, and their strongholds were demolished. They had no home to return to in either of us.

The places that were emptied were filled with the opposite positive spirits. Where rejection had lived, Kimberley and I were filled with acceptance and love. Where spirits of death had lived, we were filled with life. For every unholy spirit that left, we were filled with an attribute of God!

For every unholy spirit that left, we were filled with an attribute of God!

> *Beloved, do not believe every spirit, but test the spirits to see whether they are from God, for many false prophets have gone out into the world. By this you know the Spirit of God: every spirit that confesses that Jesus Christ has come in the flesh is from God, and every spirit that does not confess Jesus is not from God. This is the spirit of the antichrist, which you heard was coming and now is in the world already. Little children, you are from God and have overcome them, for he who is in you is greater than he who is in the world.* (John 4:1-4 ESV)

I was so excited! This time with the Hammonds changed the direction of my life.

While I had left tread marks on the road to avoid deliverance as a part of my ministry for Jesus, it was obvious that this was exactly where the Lord wanted to move me. After deliverance, Kimberley never demonstrated self-mutilating behaviors again. She was free and continued to develop into the woman she would become.

The Hammonds prophesied over me and the work they believed the Lord wanted to do through me as a part of His ministry. They would not take a donation of any kind for spending an entire day with us, loosing us from the grip of the devil. Instead, they "seeded" my future work. They gave me over sixty tapes on deliverance, along with a copy of every written document they had with them. I came home armed with what I needed for this next chapter of our lives—one of freedom. *For freedom Christ has set us free; stand firm therefore, and do not submit again to a yoke of slavery* (Galatians 5:1 ESV).

I devoured the tapes, listening to them over and over. Pastor Shelley invited me to join the deliverance team at Christian Heritage Church, where I could participate with like-minded Christians to help set the captives free. In ten days of fasting and prayer, the Lord had taken me through the parking lot experience with Rachel, where I saw firsthand the power of the name of Jesus and the power of His blood. He allowed me to have dismal failure in my first attempt to deliver Kimberley and then opened my eyes and spirit to a spiritual world that was foreign to me. Finally,

He introduced me to Frank and Ida Mae Hammond, two of the foremost people in deliverance in America, and allowed them to take Kimberley and me through an amazing experience to freedom!

While my major assignment remained with healing the sick, I realized that one can only have moderate success without the recognition of unholy spirits that cause disease. The Lord showed me that healing can often be impeded without deliverance first, as much as it can be impeded if a person holds on to unforgiveness.

> *God anointed Jesus of Nazareth with the Holy Spirit and with power. He went about doing good and healing all who were oppressed by the devil, for God was with him.* (Acts 10:38 ESV)

For years I had quoted this Scripture that says, *Jesus went about doing good and healing all manner of diseases.* I saw Jesus as healer.

After my experience with deliverance, this all changed. Clearly, if I was to be effective in the ministry to which God was calling me, then I was going to have to deal with demon spirits. It was time to add the second part of this powerful Scripture: *Jesus went about doing good and healed all who were oppressed by the devil, for God was with him.* At that point, I knew Jesus as healer and deliverer.

Chapter 10

A Light to the World

You are the light of the world. A city set on a hill cannot be hidden. Nor do people light a lamp and put it under a basket, but on a stand, and it gives light to all in the house. In the same way, let your light shine before others, so that they may see your good works and give glory to your Father who is in heaven.

Matthew 5:14-16 ESV

WHEN PEOPLE FACE FIRES in their lives, they tend to have one of two reactions. Many will run to the Lord, trusting that He is the only way through the fire, allowing the transformation He wants to bring. Others will run away from the Lord, wanting nothing to do with a God who would allow them to suffer, trying everything they can to avoid the flames. Kimberley loved the Lord with all her heart, soul, and strength. I have never known anyone who wanted to be with the Lord more than she did.

She loved Scripture and the Scripture songs of worship and praise that played quietly and constantly in her room. One of her favorite passages was Deuteronomy 6:4-5, the Shema:

> *Hear, O Israel: The Lord our God, the Lord is one. You shall love the Lord your God with all your heart and all your soul and with all your might.*

Shema is an interesting Hebrew word that means much more than *to hear* or *to listen. Shema* requires action on the part of the hearer. Hear *and* obey! The Shema told the Children of Israel that there is only one God and that they needed to give all their love and devotion to Him. God did not want to be one of many gods, even if He was the most important God. This was transformational thinking in the polytheistic world in which they lived.

This is still the call for Christians today, who live in the same kind of world bombarded with many gods. The Lord wants to be our only God, with no little gods competing with Him. Kimberley understood and lived this. She might be watching a show on television, and if one bad word was spoken, she asked that the TV be turned off. When someone has a Kingdom purpose that keeps them in a fire, that person will draw closer to the Lord—if they accept their calling. That describes Kimberley.

The amazing thing about Kimberley was the purity with which she loved the Lord and how this translated into the way she lived her life. Kimberley didn't ask why she was disabled with a string of disabilities: Pervasive Developmental Disorder-Not Otherwise Specified, Obsessive Compulsive Disorder, sensory disabilities, expressive language disorder, and physical impairment. Instead, she focused on the Lord with her time and energy, trusting His plan for her life. As a result, we lived a life of what I call "small miracles." In the fire, the presence of God is manifested in ways not usually seen by people living normal, busy lives.

In the fire, the presence of God is manifested in ways not usually seen by people living normal, busy lives.

The Lord blessed Kimberley in ways I have not experienced. Shortly after our trip to Steamboat Springs to visit the neurologist and Kimberley saying her first word, *hallelujah,* she was lying on our living room floor. I came down the stairs to find my daughter literally glowing with a sweet gentleness on her face. Her eyes were sparkling and fixed on a space above our front door. She was waving her little hand while saying "Hi" repeatedly, as if she were addressing a real person. I looked and saw nothing. I knew from the look on her face that she was having a visitation from the Lord or from one of His angels. She was enveloped with an unusual peace I witnessed many other times throughout her life.

Regularly, she shared that she experienced visitation by angels. They encouraged her love for Jesus. When she was older and able to pray more freely, she ended every prayer she prayed with a paraphrase of Psalm 91:11: "Thank you, Lord, that You give Your angels charge over me, to keep me safe in all my ways. In Jesus' name, Amen."

One morning when Kimberley was ten years old, my mother and I were preparing lunch in the kitchen while Kimberley was watching the *700 Club* with Ben Kinchlow. As was her habit, she was talking back and forth with Ben, so I didn't think much about it. She turned to me and said, *"Mommy, I just asked Jesus into my heart. I used to know about Him, now I know Him."* I asked her to repeat what she said, and she couldn't. That clear and profound message was just for me. I was ecstatic!

When Kimberley was a young child, I would ask her where Jesus lived, and she would point to her heart. I asked the Lord how I would know that her faith was real, rather than something I taught her. On April 17, 1992, a deep peace flooded me when Kimberley invited Jesus to live in her heart. What a profound statement. There was no way she could distinguish between knowing *about* Him and *knowing* Him, yet she did. These words still ring in my ears as one of the happiest days of my life! I have never questioned that this was truly the day and hour she was saved and that her eternity was settled.

Kimberley often began her day by praising the Lord. One special day was May 13, 1994, two years after her salvation experience. My mother and I were in the family room enjoying listening to her expression of love to the Lord. She raised her hands and told Jesus how much she adored Him. After about thirty minutes in the presence of the Lord, she expressed her desire to be baptized. I asked if she knew what baptism meant. She matter-of-factly explained in her special way that when someone goes under the water, it means the death of Jesus on the cross; and when they come out of the water, it means His resurrection and living with the Father in heaven.

I asked how she had come to this decision, and she said Holy Spirit told her it was time to be baptized. She asked for the phone to call the church to set it up. A baptism service had already been scheduled for Sunday night, and she floated through the next two days in anticipation of this occasion. When her moment came for the pastor to baptize her, I took her into the baptism pool. We all cheered as our pastor went under the water with her. As she came out of the water, she grabbed me and squealed, "Hallelujah!"

She was singularly focused on the Lord and able to rest in Him no matter the circumstances. This translated into a life full of smiles and laughter. Her relationship with her Aunt Bev especially reflected this. Those two could find the tiniest thing to enjoy and laugh hysterically about. One special memory for me was around Christmas time. I had some last-minute shopping to do for Kimberley and asked Bev if she would take Kimberley to other areas of the department store so I could shop without Kimberley seeing what I was doing.

When I finished shopping and had taken my purchases to the van, I came back into the store and wondered where they might be. In a moment, I was led directly to their contagious laughter. They were impossible to miss! When I found them, they were filling a shopping cart with a purple Christmas tree accompanied by hot pink, purple, and lime green ornaments. I laughed and handed her my credit card so they could make their purchase. That purple tree adorned her dresser every December after that.

Next to *Hallelujah, I love you* was Kimberley's favorite expression. She told everyone she knew, "I love you" often. Because of OCD, her brain required a specific response from the receiver: "I love you too." I have no doubt we said, "I love you, I love you too" to each other dozens of times in any given day. This became a problem when she was in the tenth grade because her teacher didn't think it was appropriate for high school students to say, "I love you." She refused to say, "I love you, too" back to Kimberley. This became a block to Kimberley's ability to learn.

Combined with this, Kimberley needed to hug and gave the best hugs. We spent many hours each day sitting together hugging. Her powerful hugs would calm her when she was entering sensory overload because they added gravity to her joints and reorganized her brain. This same teacher did not think it appropriate for high school students to hug. Kimberley started acting out because of these two issues with her teacher, and I was called in for a teacher conference.

God is so good. The teacher and I conferred outside the special education classroom so she could step into the room if the aide needed her. She explained to me that she was no longer going to allow Kimberley to say, "I love you" and that she would not hug her at school. At that moment, one of the high school girls we knew from our church popped around the corner. Ashley Caldwell lit up when she saw me, hurried over to us, and gave me a warm hug. I introduced her to the teacher, and then Ashley left saying, "I love you, Dr. Shepard."

I had to stop myself from the laughter I felt inside. God works in such mysterious ways, and He always looked out for Kimberley in ways I could not have orchestrated. Kimberley's teacher looked at me, recognizing what had just happened. She replied, "Okay, I will let Kimberley say, 'I love you' one time each day, and I will reply with 'I love you too.' She can choose if she wants to be hugged when she arrives at school or when it's time to go home."

Problem solved by the goodness of God. For the rest of Kimberley's schooling, she was put in a different learning situation with Mrs. Voyles, one of the best teachers in the school system, who completely understood how to work with and teach her. This was a fire the Lord graciously blew out!

Kimberley was a light who drew people to her. Strangers were drawn to her because of the joy and peace she radiated.

> *You are the light of the world. A city set on a hill cannot be hidden. Nor do people light a lamp and put it under*

a basket, but on a stand, and it gives light to all in the house. In the same way, let your light shine before others, so that they may see your good works and give glory to your Father who is in heaven. (Matthew 5:14-16 ESV)

Kimberley's light shone any time she was in public. She was a light on a hill that could not be hidden.

One Thanksgiving, we volunteered to be greeters for a community dinner given for anyone who didn't have a place to go for Thanksgiving. Hundreds of people were fed by this ministry, including many who were homeless. We stood outside, and every person who arrived received a hug from Kimberley as she told them, "I love you." She also told them, "Jesus loves you." Here was a teenage girl in a wheelchair with grown men and women waiting in line for her hugs! Many had tears in their eyes as they left her to go inside for a warm meal. She had good works in ways that went unnoticed by many but blessed those in need. I know these precious people saw Jesus in her eyes and felt Him in her hugs.

God blessed Kimberley and answered her prayers. We had friends who would call and ask for Kimberley to pray for their needs. She knew the Lord, and He knew her intimately. She had a complete expectation that the Lord would answer when she asked.

One Saturday morning, Kimberley crawled up on the couch beside me and said, "Mom, we need to talk." She proceeded to tell me that she needed a cat. I explained to her why that was a bad idea. First, I explained that I didn't like litter boxes and that would be my responsibility. I had a lung issue that could be aggravated by kitty dander. We liked to travel, and a cat would be a problem since we would have to find someone to take care of a cat. I offered many more excuses. At the end of our conversation, Kimberley looked at me and said in her innocent way, "I understand Mommy, but I am going to pray about it."

The next morning, a tiny, four-month-old, long-haired, green-eyed, beautiful black kitten showed up at our back door. When Kimberley saw this kitten "the Lord had brought her," she squealed with delight, believing the Lord had answered her prayer. The Humane Society said the kitty had no chip, so we could leave the kitten with them to be euthanized or we could keep the kitty. We knocked on our neighbors' doors to see if she belonged to them, and no one claimed her. We became the proud owners of a kitten.

Kimberley wanted to give her new friend a biblical name. She named her from a verse in another favorite chapter she had memorized: *He that dwelleth in the secret place of the most High shall abide under the shadow of the Almighty* (Psalm 91:1 KJV). She named our new black kitten Shadow. Those two were inseparable, except at night when Shadow selected my bed as her resting place.

God's promises are true, not just for those living cushy lives in affluent America, but for everyone in every culture. God's promises are true for the needy and for those with disabilities and sicknesses. God's promises are true for anyone who will cry out to Him with hunger.

I learned through my precious daughter that God wants relationships with His children. He wants us to love Him for who He is, and not for what He can do for us. If we could only get this down deep in our hearts and minds, we could understand what His Word means when we sing a childhood song from Philippians 4:7—"I've got the peace that passes understanding down in my heart." Each of us can have the same kind of relationship with God that kept Kimberley full of joy no matter what fires engulfed her.

Chapter 11

The Gift of Forgiveness

Put on then, as God's chosen ones, holy and beloved, compassionate hearts, kindness, humility, meekness, and patience, bearing with one another and, if one has a complaint against another, forgiving each other; as the Lord has forgiven you, so you also must forgive. And above all these put on love, which binds everything together in perfect harmony.

Colossians 3:12-14 ESV

THE LORD IS GOOD and knows that *two are better than one* (Ecclesiastes 4:9). He places us in families because He knows we need each other. Families offer love and acceptance when we don't believe we deserve it and even when we do. Families can help each other when disasters, trauma, and hard times come.

Psalm 68:6 (ESV) tells us that God causes the solitary to settle in a home. In Hebrew, *solitary* is *yachiyd* which means *beloved, lonely, solitary, or an only child.*[1] This one verse has many possible interpretations, but I like *God wants those children who are without brothers and sisters to dwell in families.* As far as Kimberley knew, she was an only child with a marvelous support system in my family, although she had little knowledge of her dad's family after the divorce. She always felt as if something was missing, despite the deep love she felt from her grandma, aunts, uncles, and seven cousins.

As far as Kimberley knew, she was an only child with a marvelous support system in my family

I was blessed to have a godly, supportive family to help me with Kimberley. My mother was my greatest support, and the three of us lived together off and on over eighteen years. The bond between Kimberley and her grandma was special, and they spent many hours together during the time we shared. Mother wrote a touching note for the chapter I wrote in *Victorious Survivors* that shows her heart toward Kimberley and Kimberley's heart toward her:

> *Kimberley has been one of the greatest blessings of my life! Her mother and I have gone through black days, gray days, blue days, and golden days, and have learned*

to praise God through the night as well as in the light. God is working within us to accomplish His ultimate purpose. How neat to stand by and watch Him at work progressively, not instantaneously.

Kimberley is a precious little ray of sunshine—loving, outgoing, sharp, a bit of a clown, and she laughs a lot and loves to make others laugh. She knows what she wants and doesn't miss a trick. I wonder what she will be when the Lord has completed His perfect work in her. Lord, we know you're looking down at us with love from behind that dark cloud. And we know, too, that a gentle breeze will blow the dark cloud away and then the glory light of your presence and her complete healing will be seen and experienced. I'm trying to be patient, Lord, but please hurry and send that breeze. What a thrill to be a part of this great adventure.

Her loving grandmother,
Margaret Stewart[2]

Families are so precious, and we had one of the best!

The Lord knew the gap in Kimberley's heart—that of having only half of her family. Knowing that her dad was alive and she couldn't see him caused deep hurt. He had two sons from his first marriage whom I loved dearly. They had spent time with us during those first eighteen months of her life. They lived with their mother in Nebraska, so when our marriage ended, much to my regret, I lost connection with the boys. Because Kimberley struggled with the rejection of her dad, I decided not to tell her about her brothers. Right or wrong, my thinking was that she didn't need to receive rejection by knowing she had brothers she could not see.

Because Kimberley struggled with the rejection of her dad, I decided not to tell her about her brothers.

On May 7, 2002, when Kimberley was twenty years old, I was working in my study when an email appeared from her brother Kip, who was now a grown man with a family of his own. He shared that he had felt an emptiness not keeping in touch with us. He asked if we could start a correspondence to catch up after eighteen-plus years. Parts of his email are worth sharing.

The email was prompted by a dream he had the night before about Kimberley and me. In the dream, he was running from room to room in our home looking for Kimberley, saying, "I don't know *how* my sister is; I don't know *where* my sister is; I don't know *if* my sister is." His wife encouraged him to look for us if he wanted to. He went back to sleep and this dream occurred two more times. After the third time, Kip went to his office and searched for my email address online. His email to me continued:

I can't say that I know what you have faced with Kimberly, but Elisa and I had Megan in the hospital for two weeks over Christmas with severe lung problems that brought us a little closer to what is really important in life. Having your little girl on a respirator and sedated for a week followed by medication withdrawal for two months leaves you feeling helpless and ready to do anything to help her.

Please let Kimberly know she has a big brother who loves her and is very sorry he hasn't been in contact with her over her life. Her big brother would like to stay in contact with her and her mother if that is all right with you from now on. If you feel it would be best for you/don't want to respond I will understand.

As I read this precious email, all I could do was sob. Kimberley, hearing my crying, crawled into my study, sat by the wall, and invited me to join her on the floor. She asked, "Did you get a troubling email, Mommy? Do you want to tell me about it?"

I explained these were happy tears, but I couldn't tell her about it yet. She had acute discernment and asked if it was about her daddy. I assured her it wasn't, but that I had heard from a long-lost friend. I promised to let her know about the email when the time was right. Satisfied, she returned to her room, and I responded to Kip.

My reply to Kip basically said that I could not let him come back into her life unless I knew it was going to be an "until death do us part" kind of connection. She didn't know she had brothers, so if they came back into her life and left again, it would be devastating to her. I then shared about each of her five disabilities, making sure Kip understood she was not what the world called "normal."

He replied with a touching email saying he didn't care what her problems were. He wanted to know his sister and be a permanent part of her life. He shared that his wife Elisa was working on her doctorate in diagnosing special needs children. Having a sister with special needs was no problem for them.

A few years earlier, Kimberley and I were studying the Ten Commandments. When we came to the fifth commandment, we hit a wall. *Honor your father and your mother, that your days may be long on the earth* (Exodus 20:12 KJV). She asked how she was supposed to honor Darrell since she didn't know him. We prayed about it and decided the best and only way she could honor him was to pray for his salvation. We figured that if he ever returned to Jesus as his Savior, he would want to have a relationship with his daughter. It never crossed my mind that her brother Kip was the one who would be saved and, as a result, be led to reconnect with his sister.

Satisfied that he was the "real deal" and that he wanted to know Kimberley just the way she was, I agreed to a meeting. We also reconnected with John, her other brother. We had a vacation planned in August that ended in Houston. The drive took us near where Kip lived with his wife and two children, so we made plans to spend a few days together. We were headed to Virginia first to celebrate my aunt's eighty-fifth birthday. We made plans to visit John and his family en-route to the party and then head west for a family wedding in Oklahoma.

Satisfied that he was the "real deal" ... , I agreed to a meeting.

Kip apologized several times for not keeping in touch with us. He was only thirteen at the time of the divorce, and the responsibility was mine, not his. He was full of apologies, and I realized that it was I who should be apologizing to him.

These sentences in his email touched me:

I guess it takes growing up and for me the power of the Holy Spirit to drive me to do what is right. I too am now feeling great joy at getting in contact with you!

... I can't wait to continue our correspondence and eventually to meet up with you and Kimberley again. We have a lot of catching up to do. I guarantee that my relationship with Kimberley will be a "till death do us part" relationship. I can't begin to thank you enough for giving me a chance to get to know you again.

Broken relationships can always be mended when both parties are willing and directed by the power of the Holy Spirit. Knowing Kimberley's brother was at that point in his walk with the Lord warmed my heart. We forgave each other, and a powerful family bond was reestablished. *And above all these put on love, which binds everything together in perfect harmony* (Colossians 3:14 ESV).

I couldn't wait any longer, so after dinner Mother and I took communion into Kimberley's room, and we shared it as a family. When I told her that she had two loving big brothers, Kip and John, who wanted to get to know her, she started laughing uncontrollably. A moment later she started crying overwhelmingly. Her emotions fluctuated over the next few minutes from one state to another as she praised the Lord for "finding her big brothers."

We went through the pages of her photo album that contained many pictures of her brothers during the first eighteen months of her life. She took the framed picture of her with her brothers, and hugged it, saying "Hallelujah," "WOW," "What a miracle. I have two big brothers!" "Hey, brother Kip and brother John, I adore you. I'll never get you out of my mind and my heart." For weeks, she told everyone she saw, "I have two blood brothers who love me!"

The trip to visit her two brothers filled a void that brought healing in Kimberley's heart. Even though I had not told her she had brothers, her spirit knew. She had told me for years that she wanted a brother. The joy that was a natural part of her being was magnified. She helped me choose eighty pictures representative of her life to include in a photo book for her brothers. The realization she was an aunt with five nieces and nephews unleashed something

Even though I had not told her she had brothers, her spirit knew.

in her that made her feel like an adult, although emotionally she was more like thirteen than twenty.

The Lord activated Psalm 68:6 in her life. The solitary child with no brothers or sisters found herself placed in a larger family that included two blood brothers with wives and children. Whether families are blood related or ones the Lord brings into our lives, we all need to belong and feel loved.

Throughout the fall, we connected with both brothers on a regular basis. We drove to Atlanta to visit John, Jana, and their three children on December 15 to spend a delightful day at the Fernbank Science Museum. On the way home the next day, we stopped at a toy store south of Atlanta. While we were in the store, my phone rang. I answered and a police officer asked if I was sitting down. He informed me that my mother had been in a bad accident and that I needed to get to the hospital as quickly as possible in Thomasville. We were three hours away.

We hurried to the van to start a painful drive home. I shared with Kimberley what had happened as I sped down the interstate. I called a friend to ask that she go to the hospital to be with Mother until I could get there. Calls to the hospital were unfruitful and frustrating when they said she wasn't there—not in a room and not in the

ER. I asked my pastor to find out what was going on and call me back. He called a few minutes later, telling me to slow down and drive safely. He said that the night before, Mother and her two friends had been hit by a drunk driver. All three were killed instantly.

I told Kimberley that her grandma was in heaven. She replied with one of the most profound statements about death I have ever heard. The first words out of her mouth were, "It's a hallelujah for Grandma, but it's not a hallelujah for me!" Over the next few days leading to Mother's funeral, Kimberley completed that statement by turning it into a poem for her Grandma:

It's a hallelujah for Grandma,
but it's not a hallelujah for me.
It's a hallelujah for Grandma,
but my heart is empty.
It's a hallelujah for Grandma,
'cause she's with the Prince of Peace.
It's a hallelujah for Grandma,
her soul has been released.

Mother's death was one of the saddest times of my life. As adults who shared in Kimberley's care, we had become best friends, prayer partners, confidants, and so much more. Her loss was devastating to Kimberley and to me, and we each grieved in our own ways. Kimberley was twenty and would finish high school in the spring. (Special education students can attend high school until they are twenty-one.) We were about to face changes I could only imagine.

We were facing another fire!

The Lord brought John and Kip into our lives at a perfect time. The Lord knew that Mother's time on earth was going to end on December 15, 2002, and three months earlier He had let Kimberley meet her two brothers and add them to the rest of her family support. While they could never replace her grandma, they filled an emptiness in her soul. The freshness of their recent entry back into our lives created excitement in her. They may never know how important they were to Kimberley during those days, as were the rest of our Texas family.

During 2002, we faced the trial of the young lady, Bethany, who had been driving the car that killed mother and her two friends. I was asked to speak in court on behalf of the three families, and the judge asked how long I thought Bethany should serve. After hearing my statement, he gave a sentence that was substantially different from my recommendation. She was sentenced to fifty-two days in jail to be served on twenty-six weekends, along with some community service. It horrified me that she was given only seventeen days for each person she had killed. My heart cried that the justice system let the victims down.

Bethany chose to serve her fifty-two days consecutively and was free after less than two months. I asked the court if Kimberley and I could meet with her, and the court agreed. Arrangements were made for us to meet in the Thomasville Rose Garden. My sister, Beverley, was visiting her daughter in Atlanta, so she drove down to join us that day.

"Jesus loves you, and I love you, too. Give me a hug."

Bethany was sitting in an arbor in the middle of the roses with a representative from the court who happened to be a friend who was a member of our church. I was surprised at how beautiful she was. Kimberley asked to speak first, and she wheeled her chair over to Bethany. She put her hands out toward her and demanded, "Hold my hands."

Her next statement to Bethany was, "I want to know why you were drunk that night." Bethany explained why and humbly said there was no excuse other than her addiction to prescription and non-prescription drugs. Kimberley then said, "I forgive you, (long pause) and so does Jesus." Both Bethany and Kimberley were tearing up at this point. After another long pause, Kimberley said, "Jesus loves you, and I love you, too. Give me a hug." They hugged for what seemed like ten minutes.

The court representative took Kimberley for a walk through the rose garden while Bev and I talked with Bethany for over an hour. We asked her about her relationship with the Lord. She shared that she had asked for a Bible the first night she was in jail. Over the next few days, she asked Jesus to be her Savior and Lord. Her faith seemed real, and we rejoiced with her, answering some of the questions she had. She had connected with a local church and was in a support group for addicts who were newly converted to the Lord.

Bev and I were able to tell her about our mother. We shared what a precious lady she was and how huge her loss was to our family, especially to Kimberley. At the end of our time together, I shared that our mother would have freely given her life for Bethany if it meant that she would accept Jesus as her Savior—BUT our mother's death would be in vain if Bethany did not walk this out and remain drug free in her walk with the Lord.

We took lots of pictures with Bethany and promised to stay in touch. I left the rose garden that day with a freedom in my heart. While I had forgiven her and the judge earlier, speaking forgiveness to her gave Bev, Kimberley, and me a Shalom peace. I understood the marvelous Scripture that says,

> *Do not be anxious about anything, but in everything by prayer and supplication with thanksgiving let your requests be made known to God. And* ***the peace of God, which surpasses all understanding****, will guard your hearts and your minds in Christ Jesus.* (Philippians 4:6-7 ESV)

Knowing that Bethany had been saved during her fifty-two days in jail freed me from the resentment I had toward the judge and toward Bethany because she had received such a light sentence.

We have seen Bethany many times in the grocery store following this encounter. Each time, she has rushed over to us, hugged us, and shared how she was doing. We met her children and felt as if we had a new friend.

The Lord tells us to forgive and release those who harm us as an intentional act of our will. The memory may never completely go away, but it won't have a hold on you once you forgive in your heart. Our forgiveness set the captive free. I realized that Bethany was not the only captive. Bev, Kimberley, and I were also held captive if we held anything against her in our hearts.

My parents often told us as we were growing up that to forgive is to give yourself a gift. We received that gift!

Chapter 12

When Answers Don't Come

He heals the brokenhearted and binds up their wounds.

Psalm 147:3 CJB

IN 2010, KIMBERLEY STARTED having fevers that went up and down throughout the day. The doctors asked me to take her temperature three times a day to see if we could detect a pattern when the fevers spiked. After analysis by several medical people, we could find only one pattern or cause for the fevers. The fever spiked when she sat up and lessened when she lay down, but they never went away fully.

For three-and-a-half years, the fevers tormented Kimberley, making her want to lie still much of the time in a quiet environment. Most of our time was spent at home where she could lie on a pallet in our family room during the day. She wanted to be where I was, so we moved our headquarters to that room. When she wasn't sleeping, Kimberley played Tetris and listened to worship music that was so soft it was almost inaudible to me. She could hear it because of her sensitive hearing.

We needed answers, and many prayer warriors interceded for us. Aunt Nancy was a strong prayer warrior, and we called on her regularly. She and my brother, David, always stood ready to do battle for Kimberley. Uncle Jim and Aunt Bev both had prayer groups that joined them in combat for Kimberley. Their churches, along with my church family and intercessor friends continued to war for Kimberley's healing. A familiar friend was James 5:15-16 that says, the *effectual fervent prayer of a righteous man availeth much* (KJV). Another version says,

> *The prayer offered with trust will heal the one who is ill—the Lord will restore his health; and if he has committed sins, he will be forgiven. Therefore, openly acknowledge your sins to one another, and pray for each other, so that you may be healed. The prayer of a righteous person is powerful and effective.* (CJB)

I fully believed Kimberley was going to be healed.

During three trips to the Mayo Clinic in Jacksonville and untold visits to doctors in town, Kimberley was tested for everything imaginable. Some of the best doctors we could find came up with no explanation for her fevers and headaches. Eventually her doctors stated that her healing would be a miracle or it wouldn't happen. After months of testing, the doctors told me to medicate her symptoms and pray she would be healed. Healing miracles were familiar to us, and I continued to pray and believe for a miracle.

June 15, 2013, was a particularly stressful day. The unbearable headaches were causing Kimberley extreme nausea. Around 4 p.m., she had the first seizure she had ever had. For a couple of minutes, I held her and commanded the shaking to stop. When the seizure stopped, she was unconscious. I laid her on the floor and hugged her tight as I dialed 911. I begged her to say something! She opened her eyes and spoke her last words, "Mommy—I love you," as she became unconscious again.

At the hospital, the doctors ran tests that showed the seizure was the result of a ruptured aneurysm that exploded in her brain. Other things began to make sense. Sitting caused the aneurysm to bulge, resulting in spiked fever. When she lay down, the aneurysm didn't bulge, so the fever lessened. The tests didn't show an aneurysm because she was always lying down when brain images were made.

Over the next seventeen hours, we fought for her life. I remained by her side and watched her in intensive care with a ventilator to help her breathe, praying for a miracle.

I expected that she would be totally healed on this earth. None of this made sense to me. Indeed, the doctor who took care of Kimberley throughout the night told one of my doctors that she expected to read in our local paper that I had been found in a ditch, having committed suicide.

The fight for her life was to no avail. June 16, 2013, at 9:18 a.m., Kimberley met Jesus face-to-face as she transitioned from this world to the next. It was a hallelujah for Kimberley, but it was not a hallelujah for me.

I believed in healing. I believed in deliverance. I believed in miracles. I believed that Kimberley was going to *walk before the Lord in the land of the living* (Psalm 116:9 KJV). I had declared this Scripture for most of her life, yet now my precious daughter was *walking before the Lord in heaven.*

Questions tumbled through my mind. What about Your promises, Lord? Your Word says that *by the stripes of Jesus, Kimberley is healed* (Isaiah 53:5). You repeated this promise in the New Testament in 1 Peter 2:24. Your Word says that *Jesus went about doing good, healing all manner of sickness, and that all who were brought to him were healed* (Matthew 4:23-24).

Many asked and continue to ask how I handle her death and her not being healed on this earth. This has been such a complicated question for me and one of the reasons

I put off writing this book for such a long time. I didn't know how to write the last chapter. I cried—a lot—for the first year. It was a sad and empty time. I had spent thirty-one years being Kimberley's mother and taking care of her. A large part of my Kingdom Purpose had been feeding into and nurturing her spiritual and physical life. This was gone.

I asked the Lord a multitude of hard questions, but surprisingly I didn't feel anger at Him. I wanted to understand how I had missed this part of His plan for her; how I had believed so strongly that she would have a complete miracle on this earth in God's perfect timing. I trusted the Lord that His will and His plan for Kimberley's life was flawless. If she moved to heaven on June 16, then that had to be the plan He wrote for her before the foundation of the world. *Every good and perfect gift is from above, and cometh down from the Father of lights, with whom is no variableness, neither shadow of turning* (James 1:17 KJV).

Kimberley is a blessing that our heavenly Father gave to me when He chose me to be her mother. She was a good and perfect gift from Abba Father, and we had a good, good life together. This knowledge helped me trust His plan for her, knowing He was working His plan through her life! Loving daddies give good gifts to their children. I knew that He is consistent in His love, and that whatever He chose to do was going to be right. I chose to trust the Giver of good things over the gifts He gave.

I still struggled to understand portions of the Word I had declared over Kimberley. The one that caused the greatest struggle for me after her death was Psalm 116:9: *I will walk before the Lord in the land of the living* (KJV).

Several years after her death, I was introduced to Tom Bradford's teachings called "Torah Class." I started studying the Hebrew language, along with intense studies of the Word in the Complete Jewish Bible translated directly from the Hebrew language.

Psalm 116:9 has a dramatically different meaning in this translation of the Bible. Instead of *I will walk before the Lord in the land of the living,* it reads *I will go on walking in the presence of Adonai in the lands of the living* (CJB). "Walking" took on a new meaning. My paraphrase of this verse became *I will live in the presence of the Lord on this earth.* What I had declared over Kimberley was exactly the life she led. I have never known anyone who lived more fully in the presence of the Lord than Kimberley. This was her life!

She communed with the Lord throughout the day. Praise and worship filled her being as she listened to it playing softly in her room twenty-four hours a day throughout her thirty-one years. Most of the Scripture she memorized came from Scripture songs. I marveled as I listened to her praise the Lord. She would raise her hands and share her love for the Lord, telling Him how much she treasured Him. She personally knew Abba Father, Jesus His Son, and Holy Spirit. She lived in Their presence.

I remember talking with a dear lady in our church, Ina Spinks, when Kimberley was around five. I told Ina I had learned more from my walk with Kimberley than anything else in my life, and that my daughter was the best gift the Lord had ever given me. Kimberley took my chin in her hand and turned my head toward her saying "Uh-uh, Mommy, Jesus." She understood what counted most early in her life!

We can choose whether we fulfill our Kingdom Purpose or not.

Scripture tells us that before the foundation of the world, God determined our Kingdom Purpose and wrote it in a book. We can choose whether we fulfill that purpose or not.

And I saw the dead, both great and small, standing in front of the throne. Books were opened; and another book was opened, the Book of Life; and the dead were judged from what was written in the books, according to what they had done. (Revelation 20:12 CJB)

I believe Kimberley has a book in heaven in which the purpose of her life on earth was written. I believe that when she stood before the throne of God, He acknowledged she met the purpose He ordained for her before the foundation of the world. She has heard Him say, *"Excellent, you were a good and trustworthy servant"* (Matthew 25:23 CJB).

Psalm 139:16 says, *Your eyes could see me as an embryo but in your book all my days were already written; my days had been shaped before any of them existed* (CJB). Psalm 40:7 says, *In the scroll of a book it is written about me* (CJB). I take great comfort in knowing that God had a purpose for Kimberley's life that she was to fulfill.

Kimberley was in the seventh grade when she told me that Jesus had come into her room to visit with her during the night. I asked her what He had said. She replied matter-of-factly, "He said I am an evangelist." She then asked me, "What's an evangelist?" I explained that an evangelist is a person with a burning desire to see everyone they know be a part of the family of God. With gleaming eyes, she replied, "Yep, that's me!"

She loved the Lord fully and talked to Him constantly. Her purpose was to share Jesus with everyone she met.

She did it with fervor. Kimberley fulfilled her Kingdom Purpose in so many ways.

One day we were in the grocery store, and Kimberley looked at the cashier checking our groceries. She asked her, "Do you know Jesus?" The cashier replied, "I go to church every Sunday." Kimberley looked at the cashier and then looked at me with a troubled look in her eyes. She looked back at the cashier and then said to me, "That's the wrong answer." The cashier finished our order and we left without another word, but I fully believe seeds were planted in that cashier's heart to find out why that was the wrong answer.

At Kimberley's memorial service, her cousin Aaron shared a similar experience he remembered when he took her through a checkout at a large grocery store during one of our visits to Texas. Kimberley had limited expressive language abilities, but that didn't stop her evangelistic heart. Kimberley asked the cashier if she knew Jesus. When the woman replied, "No," Kimberley looked at Aaron and said, "Tell her, Aaron. Tell her about Jesus!" Aaron recounted that he had never shared Jesus with a stranger at that point, but he didn't want to disappoint his younger cousin. Aaron told the cashier about Jesus, based on what his parents had taught him. Kimberley was ecstatic. Aaron was forever changed and is now a lead pastor in a church in Dallas. Kimberley's life had many ripples.

After her memorial service, I received a note from a lady I didn't know. We had met briefly while shopping at a large department store many years earlier. She had seen a picture of Kimberley's obituary in the local newspaper and recognized her from our encounter. I remembered her immediately as I read her note. She reminded me that as we passed her in the aisle, Kimberley reached out and grabbed her arm. She wrote that Kimberley said, "Give me a hug." She leaned down and the two of them hugged for a long time. Kimberley told her, "I love you," and then the three of us had a conversation for several minutes.

When we finished talking, this precious lady asked for another hug that Kimberley was happy to give. In her note, she continued that she had not been told "I love you" nor had she been hugged by another human for years. She was planning to go home and end her life that afternoon. She wanted me to know that because of Kimberley, she had not committed suicide and that, although life was a struggle at times, she had lived a good life since that day and knew that Jesus loved her.

When I look back on the amazing life Kimberley led during her thirty-one years, I have peace, knowing she fulfilled her purpose. When she had done all the Lord asked of her, she transitioned to heaven to be with the Lord. She is now running and dancing all over heaven. Her language is clear and pure as she sings praises to and worships her Lord.

Because of her disabilities, Kimberley could get away with actions others could not. If I had asked the cashier at the grocery store if she knew Jesus, she would probably have called security on me. Yet Kimberley could reach out and touch people's lives in unique ways. The Lord has shown me that Kimberley met her Kingdom Purpose through her pure and obedient heart, fashioned through the challenges her disabilities brought.

When friends ask me how I handle her death and that she wasn't healed on earth, I have great peace as I tell them we all have an appointed time to die (Ecclesiastes 3:1-2; Hebrews 9:27). Before the foundation of the world, each of us was given a Kingdom Purpose to fulfill (Romans 8:29; Luke 10:20). Kimberley lived her life in the presence of God and fulfilled her Kingdom Purpose. Knowing this helps me filter my pain, struggles, and emotions through His Word.

I can truthfully say that if the Lord had appeared to me the night before Kimberley was conceived; if He had shown me the trauma and joy of the next thirty-one years; and then, if He had given me the choice of whether to become pregnant, I would do it all over again. Such have been the blessings Kimberley brought to my life. Such has been the work the Lord has done in her, and especially in me, through the Fire that became a Friend.

Kimberley Friend Shepard

April 12, 1982 – June 16, 2013

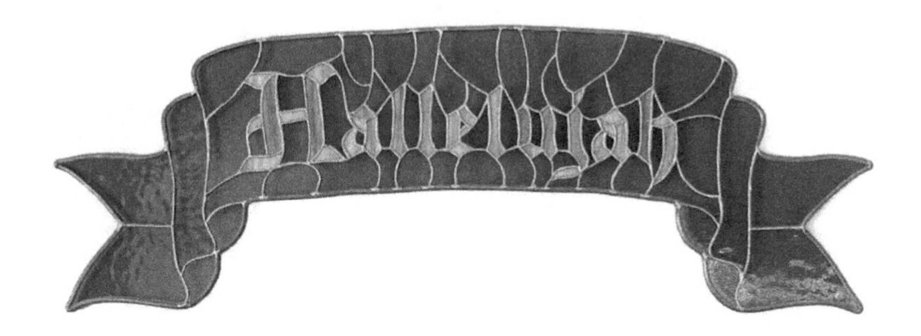

Epilogue

For I know the plans I have for you, declares the Lord, plans for welfare and not for evil, to give you a future and a hope.

Jeremiah 29:11 ESV

AFTER KIMBERLEY'S DEATH, I floundered without purpose. For thirty-one years, she was the focus of my life. Every day was designed to stimulate her and to give her the best life possible. Her sensory disabilities kept us from many activities, so our life was different from most people's lives. Yet, we had a wonderful life. Our days were filled with laughter, joy, and unspeakable peace.

Now I had a new fire to face. I knew I had to embrace my aloneness to see what the Lord was doing in me, and what this next chapter would bring. I didn't think marriage was a part of the Lord's plan for my life. For the first ten to fifteen years after the divorce, I asked the Lord to bring a husband and daddy into our lives. How wonderful it would have been to share my life with another who could have helped carry the burden. Since the Lord had not blessed me with a husband for thirty years, I assumed this was not His plan, and I had to discover His purpose for the future as a single.

My profession kept me busy, and I concentrated on it by working twelve-hour days for my university. I loved being the Program Director for two doctoral programs: Educational Technology and Learning, Instruction, and Innovation, as well as being the Program Director for Doctoral Research in Education. My students and faculty gave me support in ways I needed as I faced that first year. Yet despite the joy I received from my occupation, I knew the Lord was calling me to more than just work.

He doesn't say that all fires are good. He does promise that He will bring good from them.

The Lord never promises to rescue us from the trials and sufferings we face. Indeed, He reminded me that the fire is a friend. I was in an unfamiliar, quite different kind of fire. He doesn't say that all fires are good. He does promise that He will bring good from them.

> *And we know that all things work together for good to them that love God, to them who are the called according to his purpose.* (Romans 8:28 KJV)

We can be assured He is working His plan, even when we can't see or understand it. We can be assured that good will come from every fire we encounter. This gave me peace.

During 2013, three unexpected deaths occurred in our small church within five months. Gail lost her devoted husband, Woody, to cancer. Kelby came home from work minutes after his wife Linda arrived home, to find her lying on the floor, gone from an apparent heart attack. Kimberley's brain aneurysm took her life quickly. All three of these deaths shook our church family. To deal with these deaths, Valerie Hancock, a Christian counselor in our church, held a *Grief Share* class for the three of us, along with others in the community who had recently lost loved ones.

She invited me to join the class, and I graciously and firmly declined. The last thing I wanted was to be around a bunch of folks who were grieving when I could barely handle my own emotions. Only because I loved Valerie did I finally agree to give the class a try—after she promised that I could choose not to return after the first class if I didn't like it.

Ten of us were in the class that turned out to be a life changer. During the three months we worked through the *Grief Share* curriculum, we became a tight-knit support group. What a mistake it would have been had I not joined the class!

Throughout the next year, Kelby reached out in friendship on special occasions—Kimberley's birthday, my birthday, and her death date—to see if I was okay and to invite me to dinner as a friend. He knew that my immediate family lived in Texas and that I would be alone. I declined each invitation because those were especially difficult days that I needed to work through by myself.

Jeremiah 29:11 told me that God had a plan for me after my life with Kimberley. *For I know the plans I have for you, declares the Lord, plans for welfare and not for evil, to give you a future and a hope* (ESV). God wanted me to have hope in my future. I began teaching an adult Bible class in our church on Divine healing that filled me with purpose. Yet, I continued to feel incomplete because the main purpose of my life had changed, and I missed Kimberley tremendously.

Fall has always been special to me. As an avid Florida State football fan, I love to watch my favorite team play. Knowing my love for FSU football, Kelby invited me to watch the FSU-Florida rivalry with a group he had invited to his home. I reciprocated with an invitation to him to join a group I had invited to watch the playoff games on

January 1. Amazingly, both of our teams were in the first playoff series, and both lost! Surprisingly, the losses didn't dampen the excitement of the day.

We began a romance that ended in marriage four months and one week after our first date. When the Lord puts two people together, it is so right! He gave me a kind, attentive, and loving husband. Kelby met all the criteria I had for a husband: that he be a man of the Covenant with a lifestyle of prayer who loves and lives the Word of God. Our friends were thrilled that the two of us had found each other. A friend, Claudia Crocker, told us she had been praying for each of us to find mates, but she never dreamed two prayers would be answered in one marriage.

The Lord gave us a hope and a future with each other. Marriage to Kelby has been the easiest relationship I have ever had and is what we believe the Lord intends a godly marriage to be. We share a common faith and teach a Bible study in our home. We often teach in our home fellowship on Sundays. For the last eight years, the Lord has given us a life full of Shalom and joy. While tiny fires may arise from time to time, we both feel that the Fire that is a Friend has been kind to us as we walk out this next marvelous chapter of our lives.

About the Author

MARYFRIEND CARTER had a lifelong dream of being a wife and a mother. For thirty-one years, she dedicated her life to her daughter, Kimberley, who had multiple disabilities, a keen mind, and a contagious sense of humor and laughter. They traveled to nineteen states, making memories and meeting new friends. She is now married to the love of her life, Kelby Carter, a retired banker and missionary. They hold weekly Bible studies in their home and serve as teachers in their home fellowship.

MaryFriend holds a PhD from Florida State University in Social Studies Education. After forty years teaching at five universities, she retired as emeritus professor from Walden University. During her career she was awarded multiple exemplary teaching awards.

She is recognized as a gifted Bible teacher and educator, speaker, and author. One of her gifts is to draw profound spiritual insights from life's ordinary experiences. Through personal experiences of triumphs over life's challenges, she shares God's abundant love, mercy, and grace that He has for all of us.

Contact Information

If you would like to invite MaryFriend to share at your church, or conduct a workshop for women, parent, or teacher groups on any of the topics in this book, you can contact her as follows:

Email: friend@rose.net
Website: https://maryfriendcarter.com
Facebook: https://www.facebook.com/maryfriend.carter

On her webpage, MaryFriend includes **"Discussion Questions for Bible Studies"** on the spiritual topics included in each of the chapters of *The Fire is a Friend.*

Endnotes

Introduction

1. Phil Pringle, "Fear Not, For I Am With You" (Seam of Gold/Kingsway's Thankyou Music, 1987).

Chapter 3

1. David Ingles, "The Thomas Kind of Faith" (Tulsa: David Ingles Music, 1976).

Chapter 5

1. Karen Lafferty, "Seek Ye First" (Peabody, MA: Maranatha! Music, admin. by Capitol CMG Publishing, 1972).
2. Germaine Copeland, *Prayers That Avail Much* (Shippensburg, PA: Harrison House, 1980).
3. W. E. Vine and F. F. Bruce, ed., "Faith," *Vine's Expository Dictionary of Old and New Testament Words* (Old Tappan, NJ: Fleming H. Revell Company, 1981), 71.

Chapter 6

1. James Strong, "Aiteo," *Strong's Expanded Exhaustive Concordance of the Bible* (Nashville: Thomas Nelson, 2009).
2. Strong, "Meno," *Strong's Expanded Exhaustive Concordance.*
3. Strong, "Hupomeno," *Strong's Expanded Exhaustive Concordance.*

Chapter 7

1. Darlene McRoberts, *Victorious Survivors* (Ormond Beach, FL: Logos, Life and Light Foundation, Inc., 1988).
2. AIT Institute: "Auditory Integration Training," https://www.aitinstitute.org/ait_practitioners.htm

3. Guy Berard and Sally Brockett, *Hearing Equals Behavior* (Keats Publishing Co., updated and expanded, 2000).
4. Anabelle Stehli, *The Sound Of A Miracle: A Child's Triumph over Autism* (New York: Doubleday, 1990).

Chapter 8

1. "Wilder Penfield (1891-1976)," McGill University, accessed November 20, 2023, https://www.mcgill.ca/about/history/penfield
2. Strong, "Suntribo," *Strong's Expanded Exhaustive Concordance.*
3. Strong, "Aphesis," *Strong's Expanded Exhaustive Concordance.*

Chapter 9

1. Frank and Ida Mae Hammond, *Pigs in the Parlor: A Practical Guide to Deliverance* (Kirkwood, MO: Impact Books, Inc., 1973), 8.
2. Ibid., 10.
3. Ibid., 107.
4. Ibid., 108.

Chapter 11

1. Strong, "Yachiyd." *Strong's Expanded Exhaustive Concordance.*
2. McRoberts, *Victorious Survivors,* 219.

Printed in the USA
CPSIA information can be obtained
at www.ICGtesting.com
JSHW010418271223
54282JS00005B/10